The Implementation Perspective

The Implementation Perspective

*A Guide for Managing Social Service
Delivery Programs*

Walter Williams

University of California Press
Berkeley   Los Angeles   London

University of California Press
Berkeley and Los Angeles, California

University of California Press, Ltd.
London, England

Library of Congress Cataloging in Publication Data

Williams, Walter.
  The implementation perspective.

  1. Social service—United States. 2. Social work
administration—United States. 3. United States—
Social policy. I. Title.
HV91.W54   361'.973   79-25248

Printed in the United States of America

For Stuart Williams

Contents

Preface

The main message of the implementation perspective is that the central focus of policy should be on the point of service delivery. It is not the big decisions made in the legislature or the upper reaches of executive agencies with their intrigue and glamor, but rather the management and delivery capacity of local organizations directly providing services that will determine the degree to which those served receive significant benefits. The implementation perspective redirects concern to that crucial spot where social programs and projects get put in place and operate in the field.

Surely, it is a message for our time. After participating in the War on Poverty programs of the 1960s, I observed that "implementation was the Achilles heel of the Johnson administration's social policy."* A decade later, after a host of additional new programs and greatly increased social expenditures, implementation stands even more clearly as a fundamental problem of social policy. The claim is not that our social policies have failed but that there are major deficiencies in the management of these programs which need to be corrected. Far more effort is demanded in the hard dirty work of putting specific programs in place and of building the local capacity needed to improve program management and delivery over time.

The message of the implementation perspective is heightened by the mood of the country. Even those who would continue the nation's effort to meet its social obligations and recognize that this

*Walter Williams, *Social Policy Research and Analysis: The Experience in the Federal Social Agencies* (New York: Elsevier, 1971), p. 11.

will cost great sums of money are finding that simply calling for more spending is no longer very satisfying. Moreover, social programs are caught in a squeeze. Fear of inflation crystallizing in what has become labeled the balanced budget movement demands that the nation go slow or even cut back on government outlays. At the same time new claims such as those for energy development threaten not only to take any budget increases but to cut into current programs.

In this milieu of balanced budgets and new claims on resources, the implementation perspective looms even larger for social policy. Any new social policy directions may have to come, not from new funds but from redirection and—more to the point—the better management of existing programs. These hard decisions will require even harder efforts at implementation because people and funds are already in place. The forces of inertia and self-preservation work against change. It is not the most heartening of messages.

But all is not gloom. A historical perspective tells us that a press for new social spending will come again. *Now it is the time to get ready for it.* This is when the nation should be building its capability to implement better social programs in the future. As increased spending comes again, implementation will continue to be *the* problem unless reasonable steps have been taken during this lull in our social program effort. Hard work on building local capacity is likely both to improve our current social programs and hence provide a better basis for a claim for more money, and to support a better implementation effort when new funds come again to meet our growing social needs. That is the upbeat message of the implementation perspective. It is the basic challenge of current governance.

Let me comment on the book's intended audience by indicating first that it is not aimed at scholars working in areas labeled federalism, decentralization, or implementation. Drawing on roughly the same materials, I have prepared a much more extensive volume aimed at that group entitled *Social Agency of Governance* that is to be published by Academic Press.

This is a much more general book aimed at a broader audience. First are citizens concerned with the management of our nation's social programs, especially those who believe the United States should continue to try to meet its social obligations to less fortunate citizens. For those who think that citizen involvement is still important, the book indicates both where citizens might be pressing for action in this time of budget stringency and what they should be urging both elected officials and appointed managers to do so as to improve existing social programs.

In the second group I would like to reach are those who govern social programs. This is not a how-to-do-it book in the sense of providing administrative detail. Rather it is intended to spell out basic management direction. My aim is to present a new perspective on managerial thinking for those whose decisions will affect materially whether local social service delivery organizations will develop the capacity that I see as so badly needed.

Finally, this book is intended to provide students (many of whom may be in the first group also) a general introduction to one of the most crucial problems of governance. Here is a nontechnical, fairly extended treatment of an issue that is becoming more and more prominent in courses on social policies which treat broadly how programs are governed and more narrowly how they are administered. I feel strongly that students must confront the implementation issue if they are to begin to understand both how social programs work in their complex political/bureaucratic settings and the main issues in managing those programs.

Grants from the Division of Policy Research and Analysis, National Science Foundation, and the National Institute for Juvenile Justice and Delinquency Prevention, Law Enforcement Assistance Administration, U.S. Department of Justice supported some of the work on this book. Also, I have benefited greatly both from discussions and criticisms of earlier drafts of the manuscript by Richard Elmore and Betty Jane Narver, both colleagues of mine at the Institute of Governmental Research at the University of Washington, and Robert McPherson of the University of Texas. Finally, Thelma Brown typed the many drafts of this work. I, however, am solely responsible for the views expressed.

I
Implementation in Perspective

Implementation may be described most briefly as the stage between a decision and operations. It is the hard next step after the decision, involving efforts to put in place—to make operational—what has been decided. More and more frequently, one is warned to be concerned with implementation—that is the stage in the policy process where so much can go wrong.

The advice to be concerned with the implementation of a decision is much like the warning to keep one's eye on the ball in tennis. First, it seems so obvious. Everybody knows that. Second, doing it does not guarantee success, since, with the eye fixed unrelentingly on the ball, lots of things can still go wrong. Third, there is almost a Cassandra-like aspect to the advice: it is a prediction of problems before the great new idea gets started. But alas, not heeding it is a fundamental error that seems certain to undo any other positive steps. Fourth, and most discouragingly, however simple and straightforward the advice may sound, it is almost always devilishly difficult to carry out in action.

That is the problem. Implementation cannot be neatly segmented, isolated into a compartment in the policy process, and assigned to some special unit of the organization to be completed. As will be argued, implementation should be a major concern even prior to making a complex decision, by posing the obvious, but strangely almost never asked, question at the point of decision: How hard will it be to implement the various alternatives being considered? Even if thoughts of implementation only spring forth after the decision, the implementation problem is with the organization almost immediately and stays until the often arduous task is finished of moving from a decision to operations. And if the decision to be implemented is a complex new social service delivery project or program, the implementation stage is *not* completed when the doors open but rather runs through that terrible, and sometimes seemingly indeterminable, period of start-up in which Murphy's Law predominates.

Implementation is an extremely broad concept. Implementation issues do not arrive only with the passage of new legislation or with major legislative or executive branch efforts to modify existing programs. Rather, legislatures and administrative or operating organizations make a range of decisions about programs and processes which must be implemented in the field, so that implementation becomes an integral part of the continuing activities of the public organizations charged with managing social service delivery programs.

Not only is implementation a lengthy process in social service programs, it is an extremely involved one. In a federal agency, for example, a vast distance in layers of bureaucracy stands between the major decisions made at the top and the ultimate service delivery at the operating level. The implementation process stretches from the halls of Congress and the corridors of agency power to the point of delivery between a social service professional and a client. And along this route emerge political, organizational, bureaucratic, and technical problems, often in mind-boggling combinations that thwart the implementer at every turn.

Implementation, then, is not simply a problem of the field or a technical problem of getting a product in working order. The issue may be one of politics when local people defy implementation efforts by going to their congressional delegation. Bureaucracy may be the blockage when there is an effort to change existing organizational modes of behavior. Or, implementation may involve continuing questions of intergovernmental relationships when federal funding and supervision and state or local operations force an uneasy partnership, such as that emerging in federal grants-in-aid for social service delivery programs.

However, with all of this political and bureaucratic complexity, it is critical to keep in mind that implementation is not some abstract social science concept. Individuals and organizations must take action after a decision. "To decide" does not necessarily mean "to do." For an individual a decision requiring implementation may demand commitment, capacity, or both for execution. When the decision maker and the implementer are different, a third demand arises, communications. The decision maker needs to get the message across to the implementer. *The implementation issue most straightforwardly concerns how to bring together communications, commitment, and capacity so as to carry a decision into action.*

Actually, when we turn to large-scale public organizations, there are two implementation issues. The first is what might be labeled "implementation proper"—the effort to make a specific decision operational over time. That decision may set out both *specific objectives* such as improving the earnings capacity of individuals or reducing delinquency rates and the *means* (procedures, techniques) for pursuing the objectives. Implementation concerns putting these means in place. At issue is how to get changes in organizational behavior—that is, what people in the organization do—to reflect what the decision envisions. The first implementation issue is the process of trying to get from the here of a decision to the there of operating policy such that people in the organization are doing things in a different way.

The second implementation issue is the more general aspect of the first one. It is the capacity problem. Over time any major organization will be making now unspecified decisions that will demand changes in organizational behavior. A basic question is one of what can be done to raise organizational capabilities to implement these future, yet unspecified decisions.

The two problems blend. A major decision begets a host of minor decisions all of which raise implementation problems. Any organization at a particular point in time is likely to be concerned with implementing a decision or decisions and also expecting to make other decisions the implementation of which will be enhanced if there is greater administrative and operational capability. In what follows we will address both the immediate problem of implementing a known decision and the capacity problem of preparing for the implementation of yet unmade decisions.

THE MAIN FOCUS

The primary concern in this book is the implementation of publicly funded social service delivery programs, particularly those funded through federal grants-in-aid to state and local governments. These programs involve the delivery of a service usually by a professional person (e.g., teacher or social worker) to an individual or small group of persons in a complex organizational environment. Social service delivery program areas include, but are not restricted to, employment and training, education, criminal prevention and rehabilitation services, and housing and community development assistance.

I consider implementation problems to be the major substantive, as opposed to purely monetary or political, obstacles to the improvement of social service delivery programs. Implementation is the primary *management* issue facing the public organizations responsible for these programs. Better management demands that public organizations recast their policy approach to reflect the reality of social service delivery programs.

The starting place for considering the nature of this recasting is the lack of power—the limits of governance—in complex social programs. This lack of power brings an unavoidable discretion permeating organizations from the top through the point of service delivery. The problem of lack of power is compounded by lack of knowledge. Discretion must be exercised without a clear guide to organizational and programmatic means because appropriate tactics can only be determined in the field in the dynamic process of implementation and administration. Unavoidable discretion and interdeterminancy are the basic ingredients of social service delivery programs where prescription must start.

The basic need is for a decision making rationale and framework to shape choices that will orient social program organizations toward better field performance. The recommended decision framework for guiding action in social service delivery programs, I label the implementation perspective.

The cardinal commandment of the implementation perspective is "look down toward where services are provided, that's the crucial point of policy determination." In social service delivery programs, capacity at the point of service delivery is the central factor determining success or failure. After the "big" decisions get made at the highest levels, what is done by those who implement and operate programs and projects has the critical impact on evolving policy.

The implementation perspective shifts away from the glamor of making decisions toward the details of putting them into the field. The central focus over time is on the slow, hard task of raising management and staff capacity through institutional investment so that social service organizations will be more likely to make reasonable judgments at the point of service and to respond appropriately to yet unspecified future implementation demands. This shift in focus seems certain to demand fundamental organizational changes. Such changes are never easy. The stakes, however, are high. Inattention to implementation in social service delivery programs is often fatal to performance.

Time magazine observed in an article entitled "The Beneficent Monster" (12 June 1978): "If one institution were to be singled out as having the most impact on American life today, it would not be church or school, private corporation or political party. It would be the U.S. Department of Health, Education and Welfare." In the decade and a half since the start of the Great Society programs, the social agencies such as HEW, the Department of Labor, and the Department of Housing and Urban Development have become immense institutions charged with managing a vast array of social service delivery programs mainly through grants to state and local governments.

We'll be looking at implementation issues in terms of these grants-in-aid that force a partnership between the federal agencies charged with the federal management of social service programs and subnational governments that operate these programs. Federal grants-in-aid provide the most complex implementation setting, and hence the richest for purposes of discussion. But anyone who has dealt at the state level with efforts to change welfare procedures or to modify the juvenile justice code or followed the efforts in a city to put in place a new educational procedure or method of police patrol or different rules for using firearms by policemen will be aware that the federal situation is not that much more complicated than the state or local ones. The implementation problem is a fundamental organization issue for all social service delivery organizations. *The implementation perspective, it will be argued, applies at all levels of government as a guide for managing social service delivery programs.*

UPCOMING CHAPTERS

Chapter II will look first at the intellectual orientation of recent research underlying the implementation perspective and then lay out and discuss some basic tenets of the implementation perspective derived from this recent work. The purpose of the section on implementation research is not to summarize that work but to provide some insights into the orientation of the studies. In the next section I will try to "distill" the most important aspects of the recent work on implementation. Set out and discussed are seven tenets of the implementation perspective that apply generally when complex social services are delivered by *any* organization. A final tenet speaks to the special case of shared governance where one political jurisdiction is responsible for managing funds but a second political jurisdiction operates the social service delivery programs.

Chapter III first offers a historical perspective by tracing briefly the development of federal grants-in-aid and the federal funding of social service delivery programs. In terms of size, both are of recent origin, grants-in-aid starting to grow rapidly in the physical investment area in the 1950s and the current social service program effort gaining real momentum in the 1960s. So the uneasy partnership where the federal government has major implementation and administrative responsibilities but subnational governments or their designees operate the federally funded

programs is quite new. And this newness has tremendous implications for appreciating implementation problems in the federal
government. The bulk of the chapter offers an example of
implementation in the uneasy partnership by considering two key
pieces of Nixon New Federalism legislation: The Comprehensive
Employment and Training Act of 1973 and the Community
Development Block Grant program which is part of the Housing
and Community Development Act of 1974.

Chapter IV moves to the heart of the analysis. Of critical
concern in our discussion of implementation are those limiting
factors that over time block organizations from achieving the
desired results of social policy. What will be argued, and it is
fundamental to all that follows, is that those at the top face severe
limits to their power to influence the direction of social service
delivery programs. A host of socioeconomic, technical, political,
and bureaucratic forces interact to create bewildering problems
that reduce an organization's capacity to govern the programs it
must administer and operate. This chapter's basic message is that
the federal government and, indeed, all governments, face severe
constraints, or conversely have limited power, in moving from
decisions to operations.

The next chapter treats issues of social agency responsibility
and control (or influence) in terms of program management
generally and implementation specifically.[1] In light of the severe
limits of social agency power, it must be asked what are realistic
objectives for social agency performance. Fixing realistic responsibilities and getting them carried out is one of the most basic
issues in the agency implementation process. Once responsibility
is determined, how is control to be exercised? Here we will be
confronting the basic question of the control devices available to
the social agency managers to induce desired behavior both by
their own staffs in the field and by fund recipients.

Chapter VI considers agency resources. The agency is the place
where the federal government locates most of its staff, materiel,
and management capability. Of these resources we'll be looking

---

[1] I'll distinguish among the terms power, control, and influence later.

specifically at information, field capacity, and organizational structure. Sound information is critical to agency management. At issue is whether or not the technical and organizational capacity is available to develop and disseminate good information to the people who need it for decisions and implementation. But the most critical resource of all is people. No question looms larger than how to get enough good people in the right place to help in making the discretionary judgments that can lead to better organizational and program performance. Last, we'll be asking whether or not changes in the organizational arrangement of resources can aid a social agency in its control and support efforts.

The next chapter discusses the development of an agency implementation strategy. In line with the real limits to its power and its resources, what are the specific steps the agency should take over time to incorporate an implementation perspective? As we shall see, the decision by the agency to be more concerned with implementation itself must be implemented, and it is a most difficult task because of the size and complexity of the organization. We must consider in detail the specific steps that need to be taken. Here we draw on the earlier discussion to spell out the elements of the agency implementation strategy detailing how the agency might bargain with grantees, develop and use information, allocate its resources—especially personnel—and organize in terms of the implementation perspective.

The final chapter will be a quick look at two issues. First is the question of the implications of the implementation perspective for overall federal policy. Second is the issue of the relevance of the implementation perspective and strategy for all organizations charged with social service delivery responsibilities. The agency implementation strategy postulates continuing social agency responsibilities for the implementation and administration of social service delivery programs. Is the emerging partnership of shared responsibility between federal and subnational governments the way to provide federally funded social services? Can the social agencies provide effective management of the complex, locally operated programs? No clear answers emerge but clearly the issues need debating. And one thing is certain: no alternative strategy of funding is going to do away with the problems inherent in offering complex social services. Pursuing social goals will most certainly bring implementation problems and the need for an implementation perspective in whatever institutional framework is chosen for managing and operating social service programs. The basic claim will be made that the implementation perspective and strategy provide a useful management guide for any large-scale organization that administers or delivers social services. Indeed, it will be argued that in the emerging Proposition-13, balanced-budget world, the implementation perspective is a particularly apt approach for managing social policies.

II
The Intellectual Baggage[1]

In this chapter a quick look will be taken at what is known about the implementation of social service delivery programs. The first section treats earlier studies, indicating both important social areas that have been treated by implementation researchers and common characteristics of the studies. Then, I will discuss briefly some tenets of the implementation perspective derived from this earlier research.

EARLIER IMPLEMENTATION STUDIES

The implementation issue as a serious research question in social service delivery programs began to emerge in the literature around 1970. This is the date when Fullan and Pomfret started their review of what so far has been the most studied program area, that of educational curriculum [11].[2] Although research began slowly in the social service delivery areas, there is now a growing body of studies.[3] Major implementation studies have been carried out in the education area on large-scale efforts such as the Elementary and Secondary Education Act [17,21] and school desegregation [25], and on more experimental attempts such as Follow-through [9], performance contracting [12], and special reading projects

---

[1]This chapter is a minor rewriting of two sections of a paper of mine entitled "Developing an Implementation Perspective," prepared for the Western Political Science Association convention in March 1979, in Portland, Oregon.

[2]Because this chapter contains much reference to the literature, a list of numbered references appears at the end of the chapter. Bracketed numbers within the text refer to this list.

[3]No effort will be made to offer the reader any extended bibliography of earlier works. For extensive bibliographies in both the social service delivery programs and other policy areas, readers should see [3, 24, 31].

[5]; in the employment and training area on CETA (Comprehensive Employment and Training Act) [19, 20, 30] and the Employment Service [15]; and in the community and economic development area on Model Cities [2], EDA (Economic Development Administration) [23], New Towns [6] and CDBG (Community Development Block Grant) [7, 22, 30]. These and other studies provide us a vivid and detailed picture of implementation efforts in the social service delivery program areas.

While the implementation studies vary tremendously in approach and style, we can characterize the research in broad terms. First is the emphasis on a *detailed* investigation of what happens in the field when people try to put new programs or program modifications into place. The most useful studies generally have been factually dense with lots of information about what people actually did in trying to make a programmatic decision operational. Case studies have been critical.

The second common feature is a wide scope in looking at the interplay of various political, technical, bureaucratic, organizational, and socioeconomic factors that impinge on the effort to put a decision in place. As Bardach has noted: "It is perhaps this broad focus that distinguishes the study of 'implementation', a subject of fairly recent interest, from the more traditional subject matter of public administration"[3, p. 46].

Issues, not disciplinary concerns, thus far have dominated the studies. Indeed, a key factor in a number of the studies appears to have been significant government experiences that the researchers find defy explanation by academic theories. Absent in the work is simplicity, "that mark of elegance in the physical sciences that social scientists quixotically continue to seek" [1, p. 96]. In addition, thus far, neither a dominant person nor a single theoretical framework has emerged. Scholars have not rushed to closure, letting disciplinary concerns or a big theory dictate what is acceptable to look at.

The central theme of many of the key studies is that what happens at or near the point of policy delivery is as important, or more likely, more important, than what happens during the machinations in the decision sphere. Front line staff—those at the bottom, if we take a hierarchical view—who exercise discretion-

ary power in the *direct* delivery of services m   end up as far
more significant in shaping policy than the "powerful" senator or
agency political executive.

What I see in these studies is a healthy eclecticism—a willingness to take bits and pieces of theories or approaches as they
provide insights, but not to get locked in. Also, the researchers
have started with what they perceived as the right questions and
moved toward them with the techniques that seem most appropriate, rather than reformulating questions to fit dominant methodology or theory. This flexibility in blending the useful parts of
earlier theories where helpful while discarding the rest, has
yielded a relatively rich knowledge base in a fairly brief period of
time.

Thus far, I have been trying to spell out the orientation and
framework employed in studies of the implementation process,
not what has been found. Moreover, the discussion has been cast
in terms of research rather than social program organizations. But
the jump to these concerns is short. The flaws of academe have so
often been the flaws of the public organization—the lack of focus
on implementation in the academic community pales as compared
to that in the social agencies. There too a host of factors led away
from the right question. As I observed, based upon my experiences in the Johnson administration:

It is easy, in the complexity and in the many layers of power and authority, to lose one's sense of direction toward the fundamental goals of an
organization. In the period under discussion (1965–1968), many people
in the social policy agencies sincerely wanted their programs to help
participants, and in a general way made decisions with such outcome
goals in mind. And what could be more obvious than the fact that
these . . . decisions needed to be implemented, and that inattention to
implementation would almost certainly be fatal. But a fantastic amount
of bureaucratic foliage so obscured the way that social agencies lost sight
of this simple and fundamental proposition. [29, p. 149]

THE TENETS OF THE IMPLEMENTATION PERSPECTIVE

This section discusses eight tenets that I believe present the basic
themes from the recent work on implementation. Several brief

comments are needed. This is an effort to synthesize earlier research through some general statements that provide broad perspective on the implementation issue. It certainly is not viewed as a cohesive theory of the implementation process. At this level of generalization, such statements may offer a useful hueristic base for discussion, but specification going well beyond what we now know will be required to integrate these notions and rule out inconsistencies. Finally, in elaborating on the tenets we should be clear that much of the usefulness of the work on implementation comes from the rich details and the insights which take on full meaning only in terms of those details. The most I can hope for in this section is to make the tenets more explicit so that you can relate them to some of the earlier work.

The eight tenets of the implementation perspective are as follows:

1. The innate complexity and diversity in the social service delivery program areas make it most unlikely that effective program approaches can be developed which are useful to many communities without extensive modifications that must be made over a considerable period of time by those communities themselves.

2. The major determinant of the path of social service delivery program implementation will be the institutional *process* through which various institutional actors attempt over time to develop the organizational means of delivering social services that meet their particular needs and interests.

3. The individuals who deliver social services will operate in settings where there is significant, irreducible discretion beyond the control of higher organizational echelons, *and* such discretionary behavior is a necessary component of reasonable service delivery.

4. The central concerns of management must be the *commitment* to program objectives of the organizational units *directly* responsible for service delivery and the *capacity* of those units to provide particular services and to make needed discretionary judgments.

5. A long time horizon is needed for implementing major institutional changes because organizations generally exhibit both strong resistance to such changes and high susceptibility to prolonged disturbances when experiencing significant changes.

6. At best the broad direction of social policy, not a detailed master plan, can be determined, so the implementation process should have the flexibility for adjustments—or fixing—in response to unexpected events.

7. The information most needed for the management of implementation should provide rich details about the capacity over time of social service delivery organizations to cope with their environments and about means of improving organizational performance within that environment.

8. In the special case of *shared governance* through grants-in-aid for social programs where organizations in different political jurisdictions share responsibilities, these organizations are mutually dependent; however, the local (operating) entities occupy the central role because of local political/bureaucratic power, technical problems of exerting hierarchical control by the granting agency, and the fact that local organizations actually deliver the services. [4]

We now turn to a general discussion of each of the seven tenets meant to apply to *all* large-scale organizations engaged in the management of social service delivery programs. The final tenet applying to the special case of shared governance generally and federal grants-in-aid in particular is considered separately in Chapter III. The discussion in the remainder of this chapter and in Chapter III is intended to orient us toward the major implementation issues facing those managing social service delivery programs, particularly federal staffs in social agencies. Then, we will have a foundation for developing a framework in later chapters

---

[4]To cite all of the sources for this synthesis would be impossible. I can indicate recent pieces that have most influenced me. Of the general works on implementation, I have drawn most heavily on the Rand study of educational change [5], Bardach's *The Implementation Game* [3], the several essays in the edited volume by Elmore and myself [31], and two recent papers by Elmore [8, 10]. In more specific terms, Weatherley and Lipsky's article [28] on street-level bureaucracy aided in understanding that notion and its importance for unavoidable discretion; Ingram's paper [14] shed much light on bargaining; Warwick's study of the State Department [27] helped crystallize notions about the difficulties of carrying out major organizational change; Levine [16] was useful for understanding the difficulties of social planning; and Helco's recent study of political executives [13] indicated nuances of the limits of federal governance. Finally, I have drawn in a number of ways on my own study of efforts to implement the Community Development Block Grant program and the Comprehensive Employment and Training Act [30] and on studies of those programs by the National Academy of Sciences [19, 20] and Brookings [7, 22].

meant to aid managers in trying to cope with implementation problems.

Process, Not Product

There are clear limits, likely to continue, in our technical capacity to deliver social services. Science does not yield a clear technical fix for our social problems. There seldom is strong evidence showing how to proceed in organizational and programmatic terms to reach desirable social outcomes. In particular, we never seem to have a nice, simple, straightforward solution that is a sure fire winner both in producing material improvements at feasible costs and in leaving bureaucratic or political waters undisturbed. Those who would proffer expert advice on social programs have to fall back on recommending approaches that may be unproven, that demand resources not readily available, have threatening social and/or organizational consequences, or all of the above.

Take education. Few would argue against the general goal of raising educational achievement. However, available teaching techniques likely have not been tested out to the extent of definitive results. And these unproven approaches may require teaching skills in short supply or involve means that stir controversy, such as substituting teacher's aides for certificated teachers or bussing children from one school to another. Such approaches clearly are subject to legitimate challenge in terms of the information base. There is a fundamental credibility issue for specialists offering social program advice. Indeed, there are no ''real experts,'' in Rourke's terms:

Two characteristics are especially valuable in enhancing the influence of any body of experts within a bureaucracy. The first is the possession of a highly technical body of knowledge that the layman cannot readily master, and the second is a capacity to produce tangible achievements that the average man can easily recognize. This combination of obscurity in means and clarity of results seems an irresistible formula for success as far as any professional group is concerned. [26, p. 84]

An even more basic point is that the emphasis in complex social service delivery programs on technology per se misleads as to the

most pressing needs for advice. Since there is no single domi-
nating technical fix for all situations, but rather a number of
possible approaches that might work if tailored to the particular
situation, the central concern should be on process. As Berman
and McLaughlin point out, this has led us to the fallacy in which
"innovation is thought of as a *product* rather than as a *process*
requiring adaptation" [5, p. 38, italics in original]. Whatever technical approach is used, the central implementation problem will be
adapting that approach to meet the political, bureaucratic, organizational, and technical demands and needs in a particular setting.

Each individual setting is likely to have different combinations
of variables too complex to be predictable in traditional rational
terms. Such circumstances force a search to accommodate particular needs and interests. This is not some mysterious notion.
For example, if a complex new educational approach is to be tried
in a local school system, the combination of a particular superintendent, principals, teachers, parents, students, interest groups,
and so on will raise special problems far too complex to predict in
the sense of determining an immediate solution. Rather, any
solution must be derived by various institutions at the local level.

The major determinant of the path of implementation at the
local level is the institutional process in which social service
delivery approaches are worked out by particular organizations
or localities in terms of their interests, needs, and power. The
point is not that there are no common elements in different local
settings which allow us to increase our knowledge about implementation and our approaches to it. Rather it is that one clear
element is the need for flexibility in the implementation process to
accommodate to particular needs and interests. In that sense each
local situation has its unique aspects.[5]

Discretion

In social service delivery programs, *field discretion is both*
unavoidable and essential. A fundamental duality exists. On the
one hand, those at the top who either administer programs directly
or manage grants are likely to fear lower level discretion because

[5]For good discussions of the process question see [4, 5, 8, 10, 18].

it threatens direct, "hands-on" control. On the other hand, the complexity of the social program process is such that sound performance demands the flexibility of on-the-spot discretionary judgments in rendering services.

Increasingly we are coming to recognize the crucial place in implementation of the front line professional staff, labeled "street-level bureaucrats," who man the point of service delivery [28]. The discretionary judgments by front line professionals about particular services and how they will be delivered to those served are among the most powerful determinants of government policy. This does not mean these people themselves are all-powerful. The literature on street-level bureaucracy usually shows these professionals struggling, often desperately, to cope with excessive demands from above (rules, the immediate bosses) and below (those served). "They" may use discretion just to survive, but use it they do.

Whether these front line staff can be aided so as to have a better structure for discretion, and more capacity to exercise it, is crucial. The commitment and capacity of the final service delivery organization and concomitantly the individual persons who actually provide services are the central focus of the implementation perspective. Here the critical institutional investment must be made in managerial and staff capability that allows these organizations to exercise reasonable discretion in providing needed services at the point of delivery and to cope with the implementation of program changes.[6]

The Difficulties and Dangers of Organizational Change

The large-scale organizations operating within the great uncertainty of social service delivery programs paradoxically have both hard-to-penetrate shells and fragile interiors. Efforts that are likely to have a significant impact on people's institutional power and/or status are usually met with strong resistance. Organizational units do not like to give up resources or be pushed down in the institutional

---

[6]See [28] for a good discussion of street-level bureaucrats and the implications in terms of unavoidable discretion. More generally, the references cited in the previous footnote are relevant to the discretion question.

pecking order; individuals in those units will not yield their power
or prerogatives easily. Trying to make such changes may be like
running into a stone wall or hitting a pillow that gives and gives
but does not provide an opening.

However, if the organizational shell cracks, and especially if
the pressure has been brief and intense, the results may be
shattering to organizational morale. The reorganization or restructuring that sends people to different places or positions,
makes big winners and losers, and in general changes how things
are done, unless orchestrated with great care, can paralyze an
organization. What dominates thinking is the personal impact of
the changes on staff and their units rather than the intended
substance of the change.

There is no clearer message sweeping from the Great Society
years through the early Carter administration than that of the difficulty of organizational change. When we combine the field
difficulties of social programs with organizational rigidity and
fragility, there seems no escaping the need for a relatively long
time horizon. [7]

Planning and Fixing

At the same time, we cannot see very clearly or very far into the
future. The underlying uncertainty in social service programs
hampers efforts to plan and to act, so that making detailed,
complex plans is seldom reasonable. The usual situation is such
that "policymaking and policy planning should be directional"
[16, pp. 164–165]. The analogy might be to a group of travelers
who can only determine the desired direction of their travel, not
the actual terrain.

Planning must not overreach. In the case of a new piece of
legislation, for example, to spell out in great specificity a plan of
action from legislative enactment to "final" implementation
would be sheer folly. Rather, any plan should be a broad attempt
to guide action while building in the flexibility to cope with the

---

[7]For a first-rate account of the impact of internally imposed organizational
change, see [27]. Warwick derives general concepts applicable also to organizational changes imposed from the outside.

one certainty in the implementation process—that unexpected changes will occur and demand fixing.

The indeterminancy of the performance game leads to the notion of fixing. Fixing involves adjustments, repairs, and modifications. As a new program starts up, legislation is quickly found to have flaws, detailed plans go awry, bargains break down.

Even if a path can be laid out reasonably well (the plan can be more detailed), travelers will be confronted by a host of contingencies a planner either did not conceive of or, if he did, had no way of knowing which approaches to take until particular situations unfold. The best of game plans only takes one so far. The need in the implementation process is for a guide (or fixer) who can keep the group headed the right way by figuring out where to go and how to proceed. The call is for someone to step in and try to set things right during the dynamics of play in the performance game.

The fixer represents a crucial position in an implementation effort. That fixer needs to have the power to intervene, and be willing to take the time to work through adjustments along the way. The big problem, as we shall see, is to find a top-level fixer.[8]

The Need for Information Showing Organizational Dynamics and Detail

The central information question of the implementation perspective concerns how people do behave or should behave in their organizational role and status, that is, their organizational performance. The crucial factor is the dynamic nature of such behavior. What are staff members actually doing in using or managing their time or that of others? At question is how staff employ available nonhuman resources (materials, equipment, facilities) and what they do when they interact with each other, with members of other organizations, and with clients.

What is needed to guide implementation is information providing rich detail about an organization's history and procedures

---

[8]Levine [16] provided a valuable extended discussion of social planning. The notion of the fixer has been developed most fully by Bardach. See [3, pp. 268–284] for a useful discussion of fixing the implementation game.

and the behavior of its staff. It must be sufficiently rich to support choices about specific implementation strategies. This is the kind of information that must support the search for viable program approaches at the local level.

REFERENCES

[1] Aaron, Henry J. *Politics and the Professors.* Washington, D.C.: The Brookings Institution, 1978.
[2] Banfield, Edward C. "Making a New Federal Program: Model Cities, 1964−68." in [31] below.
[3] Bardach, Eugene. *The Implementation Game.* Cambridge, Mass.: The MIT Press, 1977.
[4] Berman, Paul. *Designing Implementation to Match Policy Situation: A Contingency Analysis of Programmed and Adaptive Implementation.* The Rand Corporation, P−6211 (October 1978).
[5] ────, and McLaughlin, Milbrey W. *Federal Programs Supporting Educational Change.* Vol. VIII: *Implementing and Sustaining Innovations.* The Rand Corporation, R−1589/8−HEW (May 1978).
[6] Derthick, Martha. *New Towns In-town.* Washington, D. C.: Urban Institute, 1972.
[7] Dommel, Paul R., and others. *Decentralizing Community Development.* Second Report on the Brookings Institution Monitoring Study of the Community Development Block Grant Program. U.S. Department of Housng and Urban Development, Washington, D. C.: Government Printing Office, 2 June 1978.
[8] Elmore, Richard F. *Complexity and Control: What Legislators and Administrators Can Do about Implementation.* Institute of Governmental Research, University of Washington, Public Policy Paper No. 11 (April 1979).
[9] ────. "Follow-through Planned Variation." In [31] below.
[10] ────. "Organizational Models of Social Program Implementation." *Public Policy*, 26 (Spring 1978), 187−228.
[11] Fullan, Michael, and Pomfret, Alan. "Research on Curriculum and Instruction Implementation." *Review of Educational Research*, 47 (Winter 1977), 335−397.
[12] Gramlich, Edward M., and Koshel, Patricia. "Is Real-World Experimentation Possible? The Case of Educational Performance Contracting." In [31] below.
[13] Heclo, Hugh. *A Government of Strangers: Executive Politics in Washington.* Washington, D. C.: The Brookings Institution, 1977.
[14] Ingram, Helen. "Policy Implementation Through Bargaining: The Case of Federal Grants-in-Aid." *Public Policy*, 25 (Fall 1977), 499−526.

[15] Johnson, Miriam. *Counterpoint: The Changing Employment Service*. Salt Lake City: Olympus Publishing Company, 1973.

[16] Levine, Robert A. *Public Planning: Failure and Redirection*. New York: Basic Books, 1972.

[17] McLaughlin, Milbrey W. *Evaluation and Reform: The Elementary and Secondary Education Act of 1965/Title I*. Cambridge, Mass.: Ballinger Publishing Company, 1975.

[18] ———. "Implementation as Mutual Adaptation: Change in Classroom Organization." In [31] below.

[19] Mirengoff, William, and Rindler, Lester. *CETA: Manpower Programs under Local Control*. Washington, D.C.: National Academy of Sciences, 1978.

[20] ———. *The Comprehensive Employment and Training Act: Impact on People, Places, Programs—Interim Report*. Washington, D. C.: National Academy of Sciences, 1976.

[21] Murphy, Jerome. "Title I of ESEA: The Politics of Implementing Federal Education Reform." *Harvard Educational Review*, 41 (February 1971), 35–62.

[22] Nathan, Richard P., and others. *Block Grants for Community Development*. First Report on the Brookings Institution Monitoring Study of the Community Development Block Grant Program. U.S. Department of Housing and Urban Development. Washington, D. C.: Government Printing Office, January 1977.

[23] Pressman, Jeffrey L., and Wildavsky, Aaron B. *Implementation*, Berkeley, Los Angeles, London: University of California Press, 1973.

[24] *Public Policy*, 26 (Spring 1978), entire volume.

[25] Radin, Beryl. *Implementation, Change, and the Federal Bureaucracy: School Desegregation in HEW, 1964–1968*. New York: Teachers College Press, Teachers College, Columbia University, 1977.

[26] Rourke, Francis E. *Bureaucracy, Politics, and Public Policy*. 2nd ed. Boston: Little, Brown, 1976.

[27] Warwick, Donald P. *A Theory of Public Bureaucracy: Politics, Personality and Organization in the State Department*. Cambridge, Mass.: Harvard University Press, 1975.

[28] Weatherley, Richard, and Lipsky, Michael. "Street-Level Bureaucrats and Institutional Innovation: Implementing Special-Education Reform." *Harvard Educational Review*, 17 (May 1977), 171–197.

[29] Williams, Walter. *Social Policy Research and Analysis: The Experience in the Federal Social Agencies*. New York: Elsevier, 1971.

[30] ———. *Social Agency Governance*. New York: Academic Press, forthcoming.

[31] ———, and Elmore, Richard F., ed. *Social Program Implementation*. New York: Academic Press, 1976.

III
Shared Governance: The Developing Uneasy Partnership in Federal Social Programs

Two factors dominate federal spending patterns in the post–World War II period: (1) the relative shift from defense to domestic expenditures generally and to social programs for the disadvantaged specifically, and (2) the increasing importance of federal grants-in-aid to states and localities. In 1955 at the end of the long World War II/Korean War period, six out of every ten federal budget dollars went for defense. Twenty-five years later the actual outlays on defense had more than doubled, but defense claimed just a little more than a fourth of the budget. Social expenditures—the biggest being Social Security payments—have come to dominate the federal budget, and now take two out of every three dollars.

Federal grants-in-aid, which link federal agency administrative responsibilities with local operations, first became important in the 1950s for physical investments such as highways. Then, in the 1960s, grants-in-aid became the main means of funding the new social service delivery programs. These changes, as we shall see, were both large and rapid in the social service delivery areas. That's important for appreciating the implementation problems in shared governance.

THE SECOND SOCIAL PROGRAM REVOLUTION[1]

Twice in this century—in the middle years during both the 1930s and the 1960s—a president and Congress produced in relatively short order a host of new social programs which dominated the years that followed. From the earlier period came the Social Security Act of 1935 establishing both what we commonly call "social security" and the federal/state public welfare programs. Interestingly, more important at the time were a number of temporary programs now only vaguely remembered initials, such as WPA (Works Progress Administration), PWA (Public Works Administration), and the CCC (Civilian Conservation Corps). The latter were the ancestors of the Great Society programs, particularly in the areas of employment and business aid. And as in the Great Society programs, the federal government was not organized to manage large numbers of projects scattered throughout the United States.[2]

As World War II wiped out unemployment and returned prosperity, these 1930s programs disappeared. There was roughly a thirty-year hiatus when the nation pursued few social goals through federal social service programs. In the 1960s when the nation turned to the problem of the disadvantaged, whatever had been done in social service delivery programs was only a vague memory.

The 1960s found the nation at the apex of the postwar confidence. There seemed few doubts that wars on poverty and discrimination could be launched and fought successfully. After nearly three decades of social program dormancy,[3] President

---

[1]An Appendix provides readers with the terms used in this and subsequent sections in discussing the federal budget and classes of federal funding.

[2]For an account of the management issues written during that period, see James W. Fesler, "Executive Management and the Federal Field Service," in *The President's Committee on Administrative Management* (Washington, D.C.: Government Printing Office, 1937).

[3]For our purposes the one key piece of legislation passed just prior to the outburst of Johnson legislation was the Manpower Training and Development Act of 1962, originally aimed at problems of high unemployment but later amended to become an important Great Society program.

Lyndon Johnson worked with Congress to enact the Economic Opportunity Act of 1964, the Elementary and Secondary Education Act of 1965, the Public Works and Economic Development Act of 1965, the Housing and Urban Development Act of 1965, Medicare and Medicaid in 1965, the Civil Rights Act of 1964, and the Voting Rights Act of 1965. *The Great Society had arrived.*

Today it is difficult to believe that "federal expenditures on grants for social programs amounted to only about $1.3 billion in 1963"[4] But after that, expenditures for social service delivery programs became the fastest growing category in the federal budget. Between 1965 and 1977, what Schultze has labeled "social investment and services" grew from about $5 to $41 billion.[5] There was, it should be noted, some change within these social programs among the relative amounts going strictly to the poor, with the poor losing ground somewhat in the Nixon-Ford years.[6] However, the overall shift was clear—in a handful of years the United States went from most limited spending for social service delivery programs to an effort approaching $50 billion, of which a good part went to programs for the disadvantaged.

These new social service delivery programs were funded through grants-in-aid. Although such grants could be traced to the eighteenth century, federal aid to state and local governments was limited until the post Korean period. These grants to state and local governments fall into two categories. First are payments to individuals (called transfer payments), of which the largest are public assistance, Medicaid, and housing assistance. In these

---

[4]Edward R. Fried, Alice M. Rivlin, Charles L. Schultze, and Nancy H. Teeters, *Setting National Priorities: The 1974 Budget* (Washington, D.C.: The Brookings Institution, 1973), p. 180.

[5]The most useful review of federal expenditures over time can be found in Charles L. Schultze, "Federal Spending: Past, Present, and Future," in *Setting National Priorities: The Next Ten Years,* ed. Henry Owen and Charles L. Schultze (Washington, D.C.: The Brookings Institution, 1976), pp. 323–369.

[6]For a succinct account, see Henry J. Aaron, *Politics and the Professors: The Great Society in Perspective* (Washington, D.C.: The Brookings Institution, 1978), pp. 4–15.

programs a subnational government may be an intermediary entity, but basically it serves as a pass-through mechanism for getting funds directly to people. All other grants-in-aid, broadly speaking, go to state and local organizations to be used for investment (e.g., highways) or for providing services. The essential feature of these grants for investments and services is that subnational organizations have the primary role in running the programs.

Total grants to state and local governments rose from slightly over $2 billion in 1950 to almost $78 billion in 1978. In that period transfer payments went from about $1.5 billion to almost $25 billion. Grants for investment and services show even more dramatic gains going from slightly over $800 *million* in 1950 to over $53 *billion* in 1978. By 1978 grants for investments and services *alone* (thus excluding transfer payments) represented almost one-fifth of *all* state and local outlays.[7]

One final aspect of grants-in-aid is important—the receipt of federal support by localities without major state involvement. Historically, the state has stood as intermediary between federal and local governments, but as a team of Brookings researchers observed:

The share of federal aid given directly to local governments has risen to about one-third of all federal grants, and the dollar amounts have increased sharply. If welfare grants (AFDC and Medicaid), which go to the states, are eliminated from consideration—as we would argue they should be for these purposes—*half* of all remaining federal grants to states and localities in 1978 go to local governments. This trend toward increased *direct* federal-local grants represents a fundamental change in American federalism.[8]

---

[7]The information in this paragraph is taken from *Special Analyses, Budget of the United States Government, Fiscal Year 1980,* United States, Office of Management and Budget (Washington, D.C.: Government Printing Office, 1979), pp. 212–246. This special analysis provides an excellent review of the dollar changes in grants-in-aid.

[8]Paul R. Dommel and others, *Decentralizing Community Development,* Second Report of the Brookings Institution Monitoring Study of the Community Development Block Grant Program, (Washington, D.C.: Government Printing, Office, 2 June 1978), p. 56, italics in the original.

The emerging partnership has two interrelated but separable aspects: the total or partial *federal funding* of programs operated by subnational organizations, and the *shared programmatic responsibilities* for these grants-in-aid programs. The rapid sweep in this section concentrates on the broad dimensions of fiscal federalism indicating both the magnitude of federal grants-in-aid, other than transfer payments, and their direction.

In a number of the social service delivery areas both partners came in with limited experience generally, and almost no experience in dealing with disadvantaged persons specifically. And the different levels of government had had precious little experience in dealing with each other in a setting of shared responsibility. We need to explore what such sharing means beyond its fiscal dimensions. What happens when two active partners try to implement social service delivery programs?

A CASE IN POINT:
THE NEW FEDERALISM AND BEYOND[9]

To see what happens in the field when the federal government attempts over time to implement major legislation on social service delivery programs, I will draw mainly on my own research. The focus will be on the efforts over time by the Department of Labor (DOL) and the Department of Housing and Urban Development (HUD) to implement the Comprehensive Employment and Training Act (CETA) and the Community Development Block Grant (CDBG) program. What follows concentrates on the New Federalism period that started in the Nixon administration and ended with the Ford administration, the period in which the initial legislation was enacted. We also will look briefly at the early Carter administration attempts to change CETA and CDBG. This longer time frame is extremely useful. It emphasizes both that the implementation of an initial major

---

[9]This section is a somewhat modified version of a previously published paper by Walter Williams and Betty Jane Narver, "The Uneasy Federal-Local Partnership: Experiences with CETA and CDBG," *Washington Public Policy Notes*, Institute of Governmental Research, University of Washington, Winter 1978.

change is likely to be a long and involved process and that new implementation problems keep coming up, as major and minor decisions both alter the implementation setting for the original decision and themselves require implementation.

Background

The Great Society programs were based on the national belief in the superiority of the federal government—both morally and technically. State and local governments were seen as part of the major social and economic problems the country faced. The hope of solving these problems seemed to lie in strong federal policies that would carry from Washington the firm message of the nation's intent to end poverty and provide equal opportunity. There ensued an outpouring of categorical programs that often were highly specific, telling the "locals" not only what they should do but how they should do it. However, since these specific cures did not necessarily solve the major problems, new categorical programs were developed and added on, directed toward different approaches or recipients. The federal government's shotgun response came to be perceived as complicating the situation and increasingly as part of the problem. Local government considered itself trapped in a welter of narrow, often overlapping or contradictory categorical programs. The high goals of social policy envisioned in the months before the Vietnam buildup and the urban riots were not reached in the turmoil of the 1960s.[10]

Discontent about the highly centralized federal role began to develop during the Johnson administration. What came to be called the New Federalism was introduced by Nixon in 1969 as a philosophical and practical approach to the delivery of social programs. Its avowed goals were to simplify procedures, to give localities more program flexibility and to shift power over federally funded programs toward the local level. The new cry was that locals know best. The initial legislation of the New Federalism was the State and Local Fiscal Assistance Act of

---

[10]I am not trying to assess these programs in any long-term sense but to convey the chain of events and perceptions that fostered program changes in the 1970s.

1972, popularly entitled "General Revenue Sharing," which provided federal funds to subnational governments for support of general purpose activities.

The second phase of the New Federalism was intended to decategorize several programs in a broad funding category such as education. Block grants combined funds from these several programs in a single grant to provide more power and flexibility at the local level for the planning and development of a program mix than had existed under the plethora of categorical programs. The first two block grants were in the broad areas of employment and training and community development. It should be emphasized that despite these changes, the bulk of federal grants-in-aid for social programs continued to come through categorical programs.

The Legislation

CETA and CDBG were compromises reflecting the tension between Nixon's "no federal strings" approach and the desire of Congress to retain some federal control over use of federal funds, although less than in categorical programs. At issue was how this uneasy partnership between federal and local governments was going to evolve in these complex, controversial programs run by local governments but with the federal hand still in the game.

The Comprehensive Employment and Training Act of 1973 combined programs from the Manpower Development and Training Act, the Emergency Employment Act of 1971 (a public employment program), and portions of the Economic Opportunity Act. CETA, now amended several times, remains the basic piece of federal manpower legislation. Its stated purpose is "to provide job training and employment opportunities for economically disadvantaged, unemployed, and underemployed persons, and to assure that training and other services lead to maximum employment opportunities and enhance self-sufficiency by establishing a flexible and decentralized system of Federal, State, and local programs."[11]

---

[11]U.S., Public Law 93-203, 93rd Congress, S. 1559, 28 December 1973 (87 STAT 838) p. 1.

Title I, the key provision for our purposes, provided funds to state and local governments, labeled "prime sponsors," to offer comprehensive manpower services including training, employment, counseling, testing, and placement. Prime sponsors include units of general local government in areas with populations of 100,000 or more; combination of units of local government which includes at least one unit in an area where the population is 100,000 or more (called a "consortium"); a state; and special areas designated by the Secretary of Labor. Most prime sponsors are either local governments or consortia.

The overall CETA legislation combined a broad block grant program with several categorical programs. Title I decategorized the Manpower Development and Training Act and portions of the Economic Opportunity Act. Further, the prime sponsors were given much more authority than in the past over the most important of the categorical programs, the two public service employment titles in the legislation. This shift to local government was referred to as decentralization.

The most basic change under CETA was the provision of block grants to local units of government. The prime sponsor had to submit a comprehensive plan on manpower services ror approval by the Secretary of Labor. However, prime sponsors were empowered both to determine the mix of manpower services offered in their communities and the organizations that would deliver these services. The prime sponsor had the option either of providing manpower services directly or of contracting with outside organizations for such delivery.

The original CETA legislation in 1973 brought basic changes in institutional relationships. First, rather than dealing directly with well over 10,000 grantees for specific manpower projects, DOL would administer slightly over 400 grants to prime sponsors. These prime sponsors in turn administered and/or operated the specific manpower projects. DOL was now one more layer removed from actual project operations. Second, local manpower projects had to negotiate directly with local governments rather than with DOL regional and area offices or headquarters. Prior to CETA, national organizations such as the National Urban League had been able to negotiate directly with Washington for the funding of their organization's local projects; CETA now meant that local organizations had to work out their own arrangements at the local level. Finally, manpower funds no longer would go directly to local nongovernmental organizations, such as Community Action Agencies, that represented geographic areas. The major thrust of the 1960s to get funds to poor neighborhoods was weakened.

The Community Development Block Grant program—Title I of the Housing and Community Development Act of 1974—decategorized the following programs: urban renewal under Title I of the Housing Act of 1949 and the Neighborhood Development Programs, which were made part of the urban renewal provisions in the Housing Act of 1968; public facilities loans under Title II of the Housing amendments of 1955; open space land grants under Title VI of the Housing Act of 1961; rehabilitation loans under Section 312 of the Housing Act of 1964; water and sewer facilities grants under Section 702 of the Housing and Urban Development Act of 1965; neighborhood and facilities grants under Section 703 of the Housing and Urban Development Act of 1965; model cities under Title I of the Demonstration Cities and Metropolitan Development Act of 1966.[12] A major initial result of the decategorization was simplified requirements, as this HUD statement indicates: "CDBG regulations printed in the Federal Register total 25 pages as compared to about 2,600 pages of regulations in HUD handbooks for categorical grant programs."[13]

The legislation states that the primary objective of CDBG is "the development of viable urban communities, by providing

---

[12]For a summary of the decategorized programs as originally passed, see *Evolution of Role of the Federal Government in Housing and Community Development: A Chronology of Legislative and Selected Executive Actions, 1892–1974*, Subcommittee on Housing and Community Development of the Committee on Banking, Currency and Housing, U.S. House of Representatives, 94th Congress (Washington, D.C.: Government Printing Office, October 1975) pp. 25–26, 51–52, 79–80, 98–99, 114–119, and 135–136.

[13]U.S., Department of Housing and Urban Development, *Community Development Block Grant Program: First Annual Report* (Washington, D.C.: Government Printing Office, December 1975), p. 3.

decent housing and a suitable living environment and expanding economic opportunities, principally for persons of low and moderate income.''[14] CDBG is a most tangled and complex piece of legislation, but this summary statement by Frieden and Kaplan captures its essence: ''The important news is: (1) there is less Federal red tape than in the older categorical programs; (2) hardware expenditures and public works are back in fashion; (3) poor people and minorities are no longer in fashion.''[15] Although the program as finally enacted ended up placing far more restrictions on local governments than Nixon intended, CDBG through its decategorizing and decentralizing thrusts still altered the basic federal-local power arrangement in roughly the same way CETA had a year earlier.

The Agency Structure

Social agencies are huge, multilayered organizations. It is useful to discuss briefly what one looks like and how it relates to the local partner. Chart 1 offers a simplified version of the uneasy partnership which can be used to consider the structural relationships of the Department of Labor (DOL), the Department of Housing and Urban Development (HUD), and the local organizations in the implementation of CETA and CDBG.

At headquarters both agencies have similar structures with an assistant secretary as the political appointee responsible to the agency secretary for the entire (CETA or CDBG) program. Below are various organizational layers staffed by career civil servants. Both agencies have regulation and guideline writers who ''translate'' the legislation for the field, and separate offices responsible

---

[14]U.S., Public Law 93-383, 93rd Congress, S. 3066, 22 August 1974, p. 1.

[15]Bernard Frieden and Marshall Kaplan, ''Community Development and the Model Cities Legacy,'' in *Toward New Human Rights,* ed. David C. Warner, (Austin: Lyndon Baines Johnson School of Public Affairs, University of Texas, 1977), pp. 294–295. Also see *Community Development: The Workings of a Federal-Local Block Grant,* (Washington, D.C.: Advisory Commission on Intergovernmental Relations, A-57, March 1977). This ACIR study is an excellent summary of prior legislation, the development of the CDBG legislation, and provisions of the act.

Chart 1
The Uneasy Partnership Between Federal Social
Agencies and Local Governments

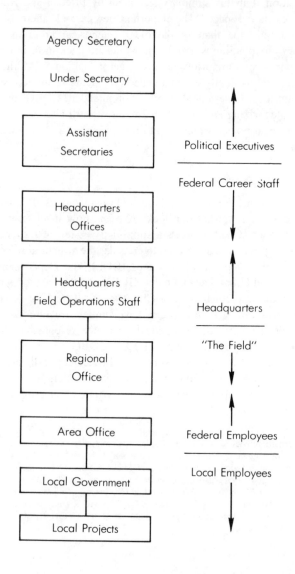

for the field effort. The latter are the main contact points for headquarters-field interaction.

In the field are regional and area offices. The latter are the operating arms of the agency with direct contact with the local grantees. Regional offices are intermediate level entities charged with supervision (management) of area offices and the provision of technical support. In DOL all area office staff are located in the regional office city. For example, area office staff responsible for dealing with prime sponsors in Washington, Oregon, Idaho, and Alaska are based in Seattle (Region X). HUD area offices, in contrast, are located throughout the region. There is another difference. DOL staff work with prime sponsors (local governments) which in turn contract out most employment and training projects to a variety of governmental, nonprofit, and profit organizations. Local governments are much more likely to operate directly their CDBG projects. As we turn to findings, it must be disturbingly obvious, even from this much simplified presentation, how many layers of organizations in different political jurisdictions stretch between top-level decisions and service delivery.

The Findings

This brief summary of findings is intended to point out some issues involved in implementing and administering a new federally financed, locally operated social service delivery program. It is based mainly on a study under my direction conducted by the University of Washington's Institute of Governmental Research (IGR) in which the implementation of CETA and CDBG was followed over several years.[16] Implementation in the field was the primary target of the study. The detailed IGR field investigation centered on federal agency regional offices with specific attention focused on their relationships with local government. ''Regionalism'' was the term used by the federal government

---

[16]The work on this study was supported in part by a grant from the National Science Foundation; however, the views expressed are solely those of the author. The findings are reported and discussed in detail in Walter Williams, *Social Agency Governance* (New York: Academic Press, forthcoming).

to designate its attempt to move federal decision making down closer to the point of local implementation. Regional offices in the rhetoric of the New Federalism appeared to be institutions of growing importance in the social agencies with more independence from headquarters in their dealings with local government. The IGR team wanted to find out if commensurate power had been shifted, along with the responsibilities, from Washington to the regional level of the federal government and to local jurisdictions.

Interviews were conducted with regional office staff, local elected and appointed (e.g., CETA and CDBG administrators) officials, local project operators, agency headquarters staff, staffs in the Executive Office and the Congress, and others who had had a direct involvement in the formation and monitoring of the programs, particularly the so-called "Public Interest Groups," such as the National League of Cities and the National Association of Counties. Three of the ten federal regions were visited in the study.

In this summary I am trying to capture significant changes over a period of years (mainly during the last years of the New Federalism period, from 1973 to the end of the Ford administration). Several key themes emerge which are introduced by an italicized sentence at the beginning of a paragraph.

Real power did get shifted from Washington to local governments. The original legislation in the cases of both CETA and CDBG was unclear and in some places contradictory in regard to the intent of Congress in passing the legislation. Was Congress trying to address national problems—that is, unemployment in CETA, and housing and community development aid to low and moderate income people in CDBG? Were these national goals the primary intent of Congress or was sharing responsibilities and power with subnational governments—so-called decentralization—the major thrust of the two pieces of block grant legislation?

Added to internal congressional confusion was the strong stand of President Nixon that funds should be given to local government with virtually no strings attached. There was considerable congressional opposition to releasing so much power over national programs. The themes of both local flexibility and federal control ended up in the legislation. CETA is a classic example of unclear legislation, with its call for local autonomy and at the same time its litany of specific charges to the Secretary of Labor, a strong interpretation of which would leave local CETA administrators barely able to buy pencils without a direct call to Washington.

Both pieces of legislation, however, resulted in a basic shift of power to local governments. In particular, local governments got more power over the allocation of funds to specific projects at the expense of the federal government. A casualty over time in this shift has been the regional office, which was originally seen as an entity gaining power from the decentralization process. Instead, local elected officials and appointed administrators took over some of the regional offices' administering duties and these offices were left with a reduced set of functions never clearly specified by the agencies in Washington. Nongovernmental and quasigovernmental groups, such as model cities agencies and housing authorities, definitely lost power. With decentralization of authority from the federal government downward, there was a new centralization of power in city hall. In some cases this meant a loss of power for citizen and community groups.

The social agencies had severe organizational and communications problems in implementing and administering the new block grant programs. HUD in particular was an organizational nightmare with such severe jurisdictional problems among program assistant secretaries, regional office directors, and other regional staff that communications breakdown was the rule rather than the exception. Most of the time, HUD simply could not get out a clear directive that was not soon contradicted by another one. But organizational structure was not the only problem. As the HUD Organization Assessment Group set up in the early Carter administration observed: "Many of the problems that have surfaced are more managerial than structural in nature."[17]

DOL clearly was much better organized than HUD and far better able to communicate clearly with its own field staff and with local

---

[17]*Report on Organization Assessment*, (Washington, D.C.: U.S. Department of Housing and Urban Development, October 1977), p. 50.

government. However, DOL was slow and ponderous compared to the public interest groups, such as the National League of Cities, which service local government. Part of the problem was bureaucratic in that communications passed slowly through organizational layers of a federal agency. But it also appears that the public interest groups simply were more competent than the federal bureaucrats in developing working sources of information. This seems especially true in the case of regional offices whose staffs often were forced to go to fund recipients to get the most current information.

During the Republician administration HUD had an organizational structure with one administrative level too many—an intermediate regional office that stood between headquarters and area offices that dealt directly with grantees. This so-called three-tier arrangement led an external management team to argue that regional offices were "managerial impossibilities" and should be eliminated.[18] If there was one point of agreement among HUD internal and external critics of agency management, it was that the regional office created major—probably *the* major—problems of communication and authority during the New Federalism period.

Agreement about the weakness of structure did not mean that all agreed as to how to proceed. The big problem was staff morale. After pointing out that "staff morale is at an extremely low level," the HUD *Report on Organization Assessment* went on to observe:

Since 1970 there have been frequent reorganizations in the field. Following the 1970 decentralization, which was extremely traumatic, there have been further reorganizations including regionalization of some functions, the realignment of the Area Offices and the creation of full service housing offices. These have resulted in RIFs [reduction in force], forced relocations and changes in job status, all of which have had an adverse effect on morale.

---

[18]See Coopers & Lybrand, *Recommendations for HUD Organizational Structure*, (Washington, D.C.: U.S. Department of Housing and Urban Development, March 1976). The internal report cited in the previous footnote was also critical of the three-tier structure.

Frequent changes in the overall philosophy of the Department, unrealistic goal setting, program procedures that appear geared more to assuring failure than success, rapid turnover in top staff (particularly Housing), downgrading actions, and Inspector General audits perceived as searches for intentional personal wrongdoings have also affected morale in a negative way.[19]

Reorganizations almost always are unsettling and frequently threaten status, turf, and/or job itself. In the case of HUD, reorganizations had come so fast and agency morale was so low that Coopers & Lybrand recommended postponing major changes in the near term to avoid continued trauma for agency staff.

However, the incoming Carter administration immediately undertook a full-scale HUD reorganization aimed at solving the big structural problems all at once. And as predicted, morale came tumbling down. A January 30, 1978 *Washington Post* article by Kathy Sawyer entitled "Federal Staffs Are Fearful of Shake-up Plans," which treated the administration-wide reorganization efforts, quoted a HUD employee as saying: "We keep saying around here that things can't get any worse—but things keep getting worse. . . . The gloom is so thick you can amost see it, and people are walking around like zombies." Nor did the big changes occur that were expected. Here is a classic illustration of the appeal of structural change, its limits and its dangers.

The social agencies did not get the right kind of information to provide help in local management of programs. One of the main complaints local government has leveled against the federal government has been the excessive demands for reporting. Under the categorical programs, the major effort of fund recipients was expended on the applications. With the block grant, however, application acceptance has been almost assumed but constant requests for reporting after the fact has driven some local governments to distraction. This has been true particularly for smaller jurisdictions that had not previously been involved in large-scale federal programs and that lacked the necessary information and management systems. Most frustrating of all in the information

---

[19]*Report on Organization Assessment*, p. 33.

requirements from both HUD and DOL has been that local fund recipients feel they receive no useful feedback from the reports. Few administrative or programmatic benefits accrue from the reams of paper sent back to Washington.

In addition to failing to obtain information that could be used to improve programs, the agencies did not even obtain the kinds of information necessary to ensure compliance with requirements. The Coopers & Lybrand study observed: "Headquarters makes no effort to assemble information that will allow it to gain an understanding of what goes on programmatically in the field."[20] HUD did little monitoring of CDBG projects to see if they were complying with federal regulations and congressional intent. DOL was more likely to check, but its monitoring efforts frequently did not address programmatic substance and often seemed nit picking or obstructionist.

Technical assistance provided by regional offices to local governments generally was of low quality and focused mainly on procedural issues. Neither HUD nor DOL furnished much technical assistance on programmatic substance and organizational viability or on raising the capacity of grantees to monitor and evaluate projects. A National Academy of Sciences study of CETA put the matter succinctly in observing that DOL had a *"preoccupation with procedure instead of program substance."*[21]

Regional office staff claim they have been helpful and can point to instances where their technical assistance was used. Help from both DOL and HUD was probably most useful at the outset in jurisdictions that had never operated manpower programs or that had not had substantial involvement in federal community development and housing programs. Often the help for these communities seemed to be answering questions concerning which line of which form should be filled out. The more experienced local administrators seemed to feel that regional office technical assistance was a waste of time. In one large city, the prime sponsor staff member

---

[20]Coopers & Lybrand, p. 42.

[21]William Mirengoff and Lester Rindler, *CETA: Manpower Programs under Local Control* (Washington, D.C.: National Academy of Sciences, 1978), p. 261, italics added.

who had made the biggest boner for the month was given the "A– – of the Month Award" which carried with it the honor of mandatory attendance at the regional office's next technical assistance session.

Competent staff is a problem at all levels of government, particularly in the field. One of the most common themes emerging from our study was that able people are in short supply. Some of the implementation problems of CETA and CDBG no doubt were the result of inevitable staff adjustments when new programs were being put in place. But staff problems were not just a temporary phenomenon.

One of the things that struck me was the weakness of the federal field staff, with notable exceptions. Moreover, federal structure tends to perpetuate this weakness of staff in the field by assigning most of the high rank, high status positions to headquarters.[22] Even worse, the field often is the place where headquarters dumps it losers.

In the IGR study we sought out local organizations with good reputations so as to be able to discuss in depth with knowledgeable people problems as perceived from the field. Hence, we tended to see unrepresentative local staffs, the best of which did seem much superior to federal field staffs. But a lot more often local staffs are run-of-the-mill needing the most basic kinds of help. As the National Academy study observed: " . . . local staffs still lack technical knowledge of the substance of manpower programs, a serious weakness that also applies to federal staff assigned to supervise local programs."[23] *Staff capability is a major problem across-the-board.*

Regional-local staff relations often were strained with animosity and bad mouthing on both sides. The conflict between regional offices representing the federal government and local officials is not surprising. Experienced federal bureaucrats were often frustrated in their efforts to break in a new program with inexperienced (and frequently changing) local staffs. Legiti-

---

[22]Coopers & Lybrand, p. 10.
[23]Mirengoff and Rindler, p. 263.

mately, regional staff charged that certain local government complaints should be directed to Congress either because allocated funds were inadequate or legislation was unclear. Many of these people reflect the view held at headquarters (particularly DOL) that the locals did not have the capacity or desire to carry out national programs. Even officials at fairly high levels in DOL believed that CETA was not intended as a block grant. In their eyes this was federal money to solve national problems and the locals could not be trusted to spend it properly. Washington officials point to the obvious cases of local government misusing CETA and CDBG monies. The claim that certain cities would virtually close down without CETA and CDBG funds has a base in truth.

These complaints, however, while perhaps justified, also point dramatically to a previously mentioned failing of the regional office. Misuse of funds must be viewed in part as a condemnation of one of the prime responsibilities of the regional office—monitoring of program implementation. Poor planning and inadequate response to community needs can also be laid at the door of the regional office, charged as it is with providing technical assistance and capacity building.

From the standpoint of local officials, the frailties of the regional office are legion. Paramount perhaps is the feeling that the drive for standardized program and performance works contrary to differences that exist because of regional variation or individual initiative. Local officials sense that rewards come from picking low numbers for performance levels and meeting them, rather than from serious assessment of needs. Attempts at innovative use of resources by leveraging of funds or coordination of programs are met by rigid interpretation of rules. When regional offices are irritated by what they consider lack of cooperation or blatant disregard for regulations, they do not punish directly by defunding for fear of political repercussions, but instead harrass by nit picking or delays. Local officials complain bitterly about the inability to get information from the regional office, or answers to important questions. Many local people feel that the regional offices end up more as a barrier than as an aid to them in trying to put CETA and CDBG programs in the field.

No finding is much more discouraging than the level of distrust between the feds and the locals, which seemed to grow rather than abate as we followed the programs. Indeed, DOL often seemed paranoid, with headquarters staff distrusting almost everyone below including their own field staffs. And surely ears burned when prime sponsors spoke of DOL.'

There are growing efforts by the federal government to recentralize and recategorize. At the end of the Ford administration both regional office staffs and local officials were claiming clear indications that the federal government was trying to relocate in Washington some of the power that local governments received in the initial round of block grant legislation. Federal staff in the regions read "deregionalization" into the shift of decision-making authority back to agency headquarters. The Carter administration went further. In discussing what they saw as a "tilt toward Washington" in the early Carter administration, the Advisory Commission on Intergovernmental Relations stated: "Of even greater concern to some observers was the action by the Secretaries of HEW, HUD and Labor to strip their regional offices of any real authority over grant decisions. . . . These decisions, which for the most part were made without consultation with state or local officials, suggested a recentralization of authority at the national level."[24]

The HUD reorganization very much represents the direction of the Carter administration efforts. HUD attempted to centralize authority as much as possible in headquarters through its two assistant secretaries responsible for housing and for community development. The design was to get the regional office out of the program picture as much as possible with a direct link between these assistant secretaries and the area offices.

---

[24]*Intergovernmental Perspective*, Advisory Commission on Intergovernmental Relations, Winter 1978, p. 6. The entire issue of *Intergovernmental Perspective* bears the title, "A Tilt Toward Washington: Federalism in 1977." In it ACIR is pushing the thesis that on balance the Carter administration is trying to undo much of the New Federalism. Although the ACIR statement is much overdone, the recentralization effort is clear.

Beyond the structural changes, there has been a tightening up on rules and regulations with much greater stress on uniformity. The National Academy of Sciences study caught the changes in observing that *"the stream [of regulations over time] has become a torrent."*[25] Congress seems to be joining the agencies in this direction putting more and more requirements in block grants or else coming up with "new" categorical programs. In our final field interviews in December, 1978 some people in the field including HUD's staff were going so far as to claim that CDBG was tighter than the old categorical programs and that most of the flexibility and discretion of the New Federalism was being written out of the legislation through guidelines. Moreover, we found a growing animosity in the HUD programs between the feds and the locals that had not been so prominent in the earlier period.

The extent of discretionary program changes at the local level has been most limited, with little evidence of broad programmatic innovations. The IGR study did not investigate local projects in depth, and even studies that did—such as the National Academy of Sciences (NAS) study of CETA—looked at a limited number of projects. However, what evidence we do have in no way indicates that local governments used their newfound discretion to make major program changes. The NAS study summarized its findings with the observation that "there has been little change in basic program design. Sponsors were inclined to continue the kinds of programs they inherited. *Few of the sponsors had the necessary expertise to improve existing models."*[26]

The NAS study, again with limited data, tried to see if CETA programs were doing better than pre-CETA programs on outcome standards such as placement in unsubsidized jobs. Comparison is difficult because CETA emerged in a period of growing unemployment. However, here too CETA looks about the same or a little worse than the earlier efforts (the NAS study calls the CETA record "disappointing").[27]

Dramatic program innovations or big gains in program per-

---

[25]Mirengoff and Rindler, p. 88, italics added.

[26]*Ibid.*, p. 253, italics added.

[27]*Ibid.*, pp. 11, 221, 239–240.

formance simply did not appear. There were some important changes as will be discussed shortly. There also are a number of explanations for the lack of change as we shall see in later chapters. Indeed, a major theme will be that we had far too high expectations in terms of the capacity of institutions to adjust. Still, it must be underscored that any hope that giving local governments the ball would bring forth rapid positive changes was not fulfilled in the New Federalism experience.

The power shift to local government appears to be a permanent one with these institutions gaining political, organizational, and technical capacity over time in the social service delivery areas. The New Federalism period was particularly interesting because it was such a key point in the evolving federal-local partnership as more and more localities were drawn into the governance of the federally funded social service programs. What we saw was a continuing growth, started in the Great Society categorical programs, of local government involvement in social service delivery programs. The New Federalism period was a time when many localities already heavily involved in the federal social programs gained more experience and others got their initial on-the-job training in managing federally funded social programs.

This intense experience with social service delivery programs has brought increasing local political, organizational, and technical capability. Make no mistake, the foundation is political power. William Mirengoff, who was study director for the National Academy of Sciences Committee on Evaluation of Employment and Training Programs, put it clearly by observing pointedly: ". . . if it came to a critical struggle, I think the political clout of the local [CETA] prime sponsors would probably prevail."[28]

The change is not purely political, however. I think the NAS committee makes a valid judgment in claiming that on balance "CETA, in terms of organization, delivery of service, and local participation, is a more effective way of handling the nations's employment and training programs than earlier centralized and

---

[28]*Block Grants: A Roundtable Discussion*, (Washington, D.C. Advisory Commission on Intergovernmental Relations, ACIR-A-51, October 1976), p. 15.

categorical arrangements.''[29] In the final chapter the NAS committee brings together the conflicts in the field with this judgment:

[The NAS study] has found that local control of programs has resulted in
tighter program management, greater accountability, and more rational
delivery systems. Local manpower planning, though still weak, is more
meaningful than in the pre-CETA period, and grass roots participation in
the planning process is greater. However the shift of program control
scrambled the relationships among government jurisdictions and among
the local institutions that deliver manpower services.[30]

The case materials provide a view of the changing American
federalism brought about by the growing importance of grants-in-
aid for social service delivery programs. What we have is an
evolving federalism that has no precise date, no dramatic piece of
legislation to pinpoint it, but which began to become important in
the social service areas amid the rapid growth of categorical
grants-in-aid in the Great Society years. And at the center of the
evolving federalism is the sharing of responsibilities by federal
and subnational governments—particularly local governments—
in program areas that either were the domain of the latter or else
were being served by neither.

Shared governance has created a most uneasy partnership. And
it is a partnership in which the negative power of each partner to
block or harass is much stronger than the positive power to move
in desired directions. Even though the locals have kept much of
the power granted them under the New Federalism legislation and
extended it to other areas, federal staffs still have the capacity to
harass and obstruct. The locals may be able to fend off the social
agencies in a number of ways including going to their congressional delegations. Members of Congress who voted for legislation which directed DOL or HUD to be tougher suddenly end up
pounding on federal officials because they got tough with the
legislator's own constituency. But even if the local government
holds off the federal effort, there are tremendous costs of battle
that drain away time and energy from substantive programmatic
concerns.

[29]Mirengoff and Rindler, p. 8.
[30]*Ibid.*, p. 279.

I have chosen mostly to look at the more bleak side of the picture. Certainly in some of our field work we found good cooperation between the federal and the local governments. Further, there is evidence of growing local capability. I am hopeful that there is an underlying basis for building a viable working relationship. Yet it would be the gravest of errors to stuff under the rug the problems we have encountered.

What I now will do is step back and try to provide a framework for looking at these issues from the perspective of the federal agency. We start with the broad issue of the power of governments generally and the agency specifically to influence social service delivery program performance. The next set of issues is that of agency management. It revolves around questions of control, responsibilities, resources, and strategy. The ultimate question is whether or not there is a sensible federal strategy for managing federally funded but locally operated social service delivery programs. Can the partnership make sense?

IV
The Limits of Government Power

We begin our analysis with the basic question of power. At issue are the limits of governments that fund, implement, and administer social service delivery programs to influence performance in the field.

In this and the chapters that follow, three similar terms will be used—power, control, and influence. Power is the broadest concept, the all purpose term describing institutional capacity to get what is desired (a decision, an action, an outcome) or stop what is not wanted. Control is restricted generally to describe the extent to which management, the top echelons of the organizational hierarchy, can *direct* action and outcomes. Control implies command, even coercion. A fundamental question is how much hierarchical control social agency executives actually can exercise both within their own organization and in the field over organizations receiving federal grants. Influence arises from inducing or guiding decisions, actions, or outcomes through various direct and indirect approaches. It is a less coercive notion than control and flows from a different strategy for exercising power.

FEDERAL POWER IN GRANTS-IN-AID

In considering federal power over grants-in-aid programs, let us start from the top. Congress passes a law. The big decision has been made. Implementation responsibilities then pass to the social agency. This is the federal government's chosen vehicle for putting decisions in place.

"*It is the agency heads, not the President, who have the men, money, materiel, and legal powers,*'' Harold Seidman has observed pointedly.[1] Although agency staff may only share top billing with several principal actors in a big legislative decision (or even have a supporting role), federal power after that passes primarily to the agency head and more broadly to the "high-ranking political executives" at the top of the agency.[2] These are the people who command the vast agency staffs administering the spending of hundreds of billions of dollars. The action is in the agency. It is these "beneficent monsters," not the White House or the Congress, that are the principal actors in the federal implementation drama.

The issue of federal implementation, then, is bound up in the question of agency power. *What power do social agencies, two or three layers removed from program operations and dealing through subnational governments, have to affect directly or indirectly what is put in place in the field? What are the barriers that stand between the top-level decision and policy in the field? What real clout do the social agencies have to induce field elements to move toward desired social objectives such as improved earnings capability or less delinquent behavior?*

This broad set of questions is going to be explored in the next two chapters. The present chapter treats the continuing political/ bureaucratic barriers that stand between the agency and the desired results of social legislation. The next chapter treats responsibility and capacity within the social agency for the exercise of control over the implementation process. This chapter is a broad picture of government power; the next one is more narrowly focused on agency responsibility and control.

EXOGENOUS FACTORS

Before we turn to factors that government can affect, we need to say a few words about things beyond the control of *any* govern-

---

[1]Harold Seidman, *Politics, Position, and Power* (New York: Oxford University Press, 1970), p. 73, italics added.

[2]The quoted phrase is from Hugh Heclo, *A Government of Strangers: Executive Politics in Washington* (Washington, D.C.: The Brookings Institution, 1977), p. 2.

ment, what are labeled exogenous factors. The hard fact is that social outcomes may be dominated by factors that are beyond the reach of any government programs—except perhaps in long-run terms where government action might influence socioeconomic conditions. It well may be that innate intelligence, socioeconomic class, and peer influence, more than what is offered in school, determine what is learned. However, for school officials, the only things they have any control over are such factors as classrooms, teachers, and materials. Other factors, no matter how important in terms of impact, really are outside the policy domain, outside the scope of policy action in that government cannot affect them.

Generally speaking, exogenous factors can be disregarded in a study such as this, which focuses on government resources. But one exception needs to be noted. There often are gross underestimates of how much exogenous forces restrict the government's capability to bring the desired results of legislation. *These lead to unrealistic performance expectations. Such expectations may not only bring disappointment later with results but also call forth unrealistic charges to the agency in terms of implementation.* Government performance needs to be assessed in terms of what it can actually do.

POLITICS AND BUREAUCRACY AT THE FEDERAL LEVEL

Our consideration of the policy impact of a social agency through use of its political, organizational, and technical resources begins with a consideration of the political/bureaucratic players involved in social policy. It is a big cast that includes Congress, the White House, federal political executives, large-scale public bureaucracies, local politicians and other members of local governments that administer federal funds, special interest groups, those who operate programs including direct service deliverers, and occasionally those who received services. What I want to do in this and the next major section on local government is introduce the main players and indicate briefly how they affect the implementation process.

Political Executives and Civil Servants

There is a distinction that needs to be made within a federal agency between political executives and career civil servants. The former include the secretary of the agency, most people with some version of secretary in their titles (assistant secretary, deputy undersecretary, deputy assistant secretary), and the heads of major agency bureaus (e.g., in the Department of Health, Education and Welfare, the Social Security Administration) and their chief assistants. The political executives appointed by the president and confirmed by the Senate are the ones specifically charged with carrying out the various missions of the agency including implementation. They have one common, and critical, characteristic: their *impermanence*. Political executives come and go, lasting on the average two to three years.[3]

Everyone else—that is, the career civil servants—come and stay. For them, federal service is a career. The career civil servants, or more pejoratively, the "bureaucrats," are found not only in Washington but in the field. They greatly outnumber political executives, and collectively, know a great deal more than the political executives. But the latter have the legal responsibility for implementation (a point we'll return to frequently).

The political executives must deal above with the White House and Congress and below with their own bureaucrats before they can have any impact upon the "real world" of the field. The implementation problem starts here.

Congress

Trouble often starts with Congress and the lack of clarity and direction legislation. In looking at a law, nothing can be more frustrating than trying to pin down what is to be implemented. Although somewhat overdrawn, the process of congressional

---

[3]There will be a wholesale turnover at a change of administration (especially if there is a party shift, as from Presidents Ford to Carter). But a change in secretary during a presidential administration can also bring much turnover. There also are lots of individual resignations, in part because jobs on the outside in business and law, *after* one has been of high government rank, are more lucrative.

lawmaking is depicted vividly in William Greider's "The Grand Bazaar: Living with the Federal Bureaucracy," written for the *Washington Post* inauguration day edition of January 20, 1977:

Congress, after all, does not really enact laws in most areas—it proposes subjects for bargaining in the bazaar. . . .

Modern laws announce high purposes, noble goals, but they usually fuzz the crucial questions in the fine print, the language which declares: Thou shalt not. . . .

. . . the whole mess is turned over to an agency of the Executive Branch with vague instructions to work out the details (actually, it is turned over to several agencies). Some very broad guidelines are provided on how to proceed (subject to revision if the political backfire is too great) and a new pot of money is appropriated for enforcement (though not enough to enforce this new law thoroughly since that would cost an outrageous amount). . . .

The political advantages for members of Congress are obvious. They can claim credit for attacking the great problems of the society—but they insulate themselves from direct responsibility for the hard decisions. Indeed, when they exercise "oversight" of the executive departments, this allows them to second-guess the tough choices which they could not resolve among themselves.

Enacting legislation requires only enough votes to pass the Senate and the House and, if needed, to override a presidential veto. As Mayhew puts it most pointedly: "The Constitution does not require, nor does political theory decisively insist, that legislative processes enshrine high standards of instrumental rationality."[4]

This lack of specificity and consistency also come about because programmatic detail is not an important commodity in Congress. Members often have little direct knowledge of how programs operate, scant time to acquire such knowledge, and no incentives for getting concerned with program specifics. Again Mayhew captures the situation: "On matters where credit-claiming possibilities wear thin, therefore, we should not be surprised to find that members

---

[4]David R. Mayhew, *Congress: The Electoral Connection* (New Haven: Yale University Press, 1974), p. 136.

display only a modest interest in what goes into bills or what their passage accomplishes."[5]

There also is a positive side to the lack of specificity in allowing a working out over time of conflicting interests and needs. Premature specificity can lead in the wrong direction, restrict flexibility and innovation, or hinder the reconciliation of national and local interests. In the broadest sense the lack of specificity may contribute to the viability of federalism. But it also can play hob with agency management efforts.

The White House

The White House and social agency relationships that affect implementation appear to lean more toward conflict or at least a guarded standoff position than one of cooperation. Presidents historically have considered themselves the commander-and-chief of the executive establishment. *Their* political executives from cabinet secretary on down are expected to wait for marching orders. But the presidents soon find out that the agency has the program action. The likely response has been efforts by the White House to get more power over the political executives, who appear to the White House to be adopting the interests of the agency (bureaucracy), not of the president who appointed them. However, presidents usually concern themselves much more with foreign policy and economic issues than domestic policy, so that White House involvement with the social agencies comes mainly from presidential aides. Presidents have great trouble following Peter Drucker's advice, "never let the [White House] central staff get between the chief executive and the key men in his administration who are responsible for managing major activities."[6]

The important point is not that the White House is likely to dominate the agency in its implementation efforts, especially as things move deeper into the field. It is rather that White House

---

[5]*Ibid.*, p. 122.

[6]Peter F. Drucker, "How to Make the Presidency Manageable," *Fortune*, November 1974, p. 147.

staff can cause early implementation problems. Further, the staff well may not understand implementation issues and offer little help in getting changes that could facilitate implementation over time.

Alliances

Agency authority and relationships are further complicated by presidential and congressional alliances with the agency's own bureaucrats, local politicians, and national representatives of service deliverers or program beneficiaries. These can build continuing wedges between the agency political executives and the desired results of legislation.

The so-called iron triangle links an agency bureau, its related interest group, and congressional supporters usually including key committee or subcommittee members. This alliance makes the agency's own bureau part of what Heclo labels a "subgovernment" of which the agency political executives are *not* a part:

The common features of these subgovernments are enduring mutual interests across the executive and legislative branches and between the public and private sectors. However high-minded the ultimate purpose, the immediate aim of each alliance is to become "self-sustaining in control of power in its own sphere." The longer an agency's tradition of independence, the greater the political controversy surrounding its subject matter, and the more it is allied with outside groups, the more a new appointee can expect sub rosa opposition to develop to any proposed changes.[7]

Another formidable barrier comes from alliances of the White House and Congress with the politicians whose governments receive social service delivery program funds or with the national representatives of service deliverers or beneficiaries. Links between Congress and local fund recipients are particularly troublesome. As Ingram has observed: "Unfettered grant provisions are an attractive support-building strategy for congressional sponsors in the struggle to build legislative majorities. The cost to successful implementation of federal programs is rarely explicitly recog-

---

[7]Heclo, p. 225.

nized by Congress."[8] The greatest dilemma for the agency can come about after Congress has decreed that funds to local governments are to be administered under quite specific conditions. Then, in questions concerning compliance with those conditions, congressional members often line up on the side of those receiving funds and against the agency. Hence, the basic rules of the game become confused.

Bureaucrats and Regulations

The agency's own career staff can be the undoing of the top agency political executives responsible for agency performance in the eyes of Congress. Bureaucratic problems can flow from sources external to the agencies, such as employee unions and ties of career bureaucrats to legislators. The main issues, however, concern power within the agency—a power deriving from knowledge and entrenched position; a power that gives the career civil servants a goodly degree of independence from their ostensible bosses, the political executives.

Consider the role of these federal level civil servants for a minute. As a top-level decision moves through the agency toward operations, the key federal actors are middle and lower echelon staff both in headquarters and in the region. One need not think of them as evil or slothful people to recognize that career staff can cause trouble in the change to a new system. The first thing to recognize is that organizations and bureaucrats have limited repertoires. Implementers may not know what is wanted or else have no idea how to do it. At other times they know what is wanted and reject it, acting to reshape a change so that they're really doing very much what they did before. In still other cases career staff do not want to lose power and so interject themselves too much into the process. With the usual vagueness of legislation, federal staff has ample opportunity to justify its intrusion. Even when there is greater legislative specificity, an adroit regulation writer can muscle in between the lines with administrative details that simply "define and fine-tune" the law.

---

[8]Helen Ingram, "Policy Implementation through Bargaining: The Case of Federal Grants-in-Aid," *Public Policy* 2 (Fall 1977), 525.

The importance of regulations and guidelines, written by middle or lower echelon staff to explicate legislation, has seldom been recognized.[9] Brown and Frieden point out: "This scholarly neglect [of guidelines] is unfortunate for it is reasonable to surmise—again at least a priori—that the guideline process constitutes the cutting edge of administrative power, the most direct, legitimate, and effective means by which public administrators make recipients of public funds dependent upon bureaucratic interpretations of public law."[10] Richard Nathan, a key official in the Nixon administration, reflected how critical are these administrative activities in observing that "Nixon and Erlichman came to the conclusion sometime in 1971 that in many areas of domestic affairs, *operations is policy.* Much of the day-to-day management of domestic programs—regulation writing, grant approval, and budget apportionment—actually involve policy making."[11]

The ever perceptive Meg Greenfield has put well the general problem of bureaucratic behavior in the August 30, 1975 issue of the *Washington Post*:

When I try to imagine how HEW or any other government agency would deal with Solomon's most familiar administrative challenge, I come up with two different conclusions that have one thing in common. Either they would involve federal regulation CR (03X-14) and actually cut the baby in half, or his contending mothers, under regulation DL-9B (15), would still be filing documents before an interagency proceeding when he had reached the age of 43. But either way, the government officials in question would have avoided judgment, responsibility, the burden of using their wits and a particular kind of trouble. By formulating endless rules, we put the problem on "automatic," and there are very few officials in this town who are willing to take the heat that goes with trying to make common sense rulings—instead of just more rules.

And why do the rest of us go along? Probably because we have an abiding fear of discretionary government and a misplaced belief in the capacity of

[9] A notable exception is an issue of *Policy Sciences* devoted solely to a discussion of regulations and guidelines. See *Policy Sciences* 7 (1976): 399–518.

[10] Lawrence D. Brown and Bernard J. Frieden, "Rulemaking by Improvisation: Guidelines and Goals in the Model Cities Program," in *ibid.*, pp. 455–456.

[11] Richard P. Nathan, *The Plot That Failed* (New York: John Wiley & Sons, 1975), p. 62, italics in original.

written regulations to ensure fairness and to prevent our officeholders from treating us in capricious or tyrannical ways. Now the regulations themselves have become tyrannical, but this comes at a moment when government officials are feeling anything but audacious and when the public is awash in suspicions concerning both their competence and good faith.

Since bureaucrats seem so inclined to lay on hands, eliminating staff may appear to be the only answer to too much interference. However, the cure of severing several layers of the federal bureaucracy may be worse than the malady, as Warwick observes: "Massive cuts in personnel . . . will lead to even less risk-taking and to a search for organizational defenses against a hostile environment."[12] To use Warwick's apt phrase, "debureaucratization by decimation" can be counterproductive at the federal level.[13] There is a further problem even if federal bureaucracy is cut back severely. Remaining are state and local organizations and their bureaucracies that also seem prepared either to do things as they were done before or to create new roles to justify their existence.

LOCAL GOVERNMENTS

At this point we need to think in terms of the long history of federalism in the United States. Through much of our history *separation of domestic responsibilities* between federal and subnational governments has predominated, except in certain areas of interstate activity. Shared responsibility has come about only when unavoidable, such as that necessitated by a river crossing state lines. The typical pattern has been for a local or state government to have sole responsibility in areas such as elementary and secondary education and fire and police protection. In these clearly defined "local" areas, the federal government took no direct responsibility and provided no funding.[14]

---

[12]Donald P. Warwick, *A Theory of Public Bureaucracy* (Cambridge, Mass.: Harvard University Press, 1975), p. 208.

[13]*Ibid.*, p. 206.

[14]For a good general account of these developments, see Michael D. Reagan, *The New Federalism* (New York: Oxford University Press, 1972). For a recent discussion of federalism issues and an extensive bibliography covering both the classic studies and recent work, see Deil S. Wright, *Understanding Intergovernmental Relations* (North Scituate, Mass.: Duxbury Press, 1978). Professor Wright

Fundamental changes in governmental relationships were brought by the congressional decision to provide funds through grants-in-aid *with strings*. In social service delivery programs, both categorical and block grants-in-aid charged federal and local governments with significant managerial and operational responsibilities in areas that had historically been the domain of subnational governments alone (e.g., elementary and secondary education) or else unserved by governments (e.g., community development). The local organizations operated projects but the federal governments in varying degrees specified priorities and objectives for social service delivery programs, indicated both program means and the process through which decisions were to be made at the local level, and assessed how locally operated projects performed.

Grants-in-aid that establish a milieu of shared governance seem certain to continue. Congress (or the nation) has rejected specifically either social service delivery programs operated *directly* by the federal government itself (e.g., as Social Security offices are) or federal funds to state and local governments to operate these programs without federal involvement (with "no strings attached").

Congress seems likely to oscillate between philosophies of greater federal involvement, as was the case in President Johnson's Great Society programs, and less federal involvement, as was the case under President Nixon's New Federalism. Indeed, the oscillation is often a key factor. Such shifts greatly complicate the issue of responsibility and authority between the federal and subnational governments. In all these swings, however, significant amounts of responsibility will continue to be shared by the federal and local levels. *The uneasy partnership in social service delivery programs is here to stay.*

We are in the midst of a dramatic transformation of American federalism that was not much discussed during its early formative years, after the Korean War, and now is far from fully perceived.

---

makes interesting distinctions between federalism and intergovernmental relations seeing the latter as a much less "loaded" term because of the many past uses of the word federalism (see his discussion at pp. 16–19). For our purposes, however, the traditional term of federalism seems more appropriate.

David Walker has put it well in this observation:

> . . . there has been the steady erosion of any real distinctions between what is a state and local issue and what is a federal concern. The last genuine efforts to debate and define national purposes and aid programs in a constitutional context took place in the 1950s and early 1960s. The need to defend or rationalize new federal assistance efforts vanished in the mid-1960s with enactment of a wide range of aid programs (over 240) by the 89th and 90th Congresses, several of which involved wholly new departures for the national government and some of which were novel to any government. While many of these were limited in their scope and appropriations, the "legitimacy barrier" had fallen. Hence, subsequent actions in these program areas, while frequently more expensive, intrusive, and specialized, were not viewed as major departures from the largely collaborative and simple purposes of the initial legislation. Instead, they were treated largely as mere extensions of the original enactments.

> In the 1970s, the federal influence spread still further through involvement in more and more subfunctional areas, new regulatory thrusts, sustained stimulation of greater state and local program and personnel endeavors, and greater efforts to achieve more supervisory authority. As a result of this increased federal activity, the bounds of the national government's current domestic agenda span issues of concern to neighborhood, municipal, or county councils, state legislatures, and the U.N. General Assembly—with concerns of a national legislative body occasionally sandwiched in.[15]

Shared responsibility is now woven tightly into the fabric of American federalism.

Power Gained

One of the most critical changes over time since social service grants-in-aid ushered in the Great Society years has been the shift in real power balance toward local governments. The social agencies had immediate bargaining advantages. First, the philosophy of federal activism was in vogue. Second, federal staffs usually were superior in skills and experience. Third, the grantor generally has maximum clout at the outset of a grant. Ingram

---

[15]David Walker, "The Balanced Budget Movement: A Political Perspective," *Intergovernmental Perspective*, 5 (Spring 1979), 17.

points out: "The leverage that comes from this potential power [of fund cutoff] is most credible in the early stages of a grant program, before a routine and pattern of expectations has been established."[16]

Over time advantages began to move toward the locals. This was so in part because the locals became relatively favored ideologically in the shift from the Great Society to the New Federalism. In the Nixon administration both general revenue sharing and block grants intensified the movement toward increased local political power vis-à-vis the federal government, which had started gaining momentum in the categorical program days. Perhaps even more important, local governments and their national interest groups (e.g., Conference of Mayors) got on-the-job training in the specifics of particular program areas. Local staffs became specialists in social areas with both general knowledge about programs and specific knowledge about their projects.

We now seem to be experiencing what may strike one as a strange phenomenon. At fund renewal time, the burden of proof might be expected to rest with the local entity, to show funding should be continued. *However, once granted, the funds appear to "belong" to the local government.* Without new national level distributional decisions, the agency has to make a strong case to undo continued funding at the same level or higher. There is then what can be termed a "lock-in effect." The social agency has limited leverage over the federal grants-in-aid it is charged with administering.

The genie of local power vis-à-vis the federal government clearly is out of the bottle. The bargaining advantages that federal bureaucrats previously had will not be restored except in the unlikely case of severe political or economic changes. The intensified events of the last several years have brought local political/bureaucratic capacity and clout to too high a level for that.

Power Threatened

Gaining power vis-à-vis the federal government is not the last step for local government, however. These governments find that their

---

[16]Ingram, pp. 509–510.

capacity to exercise power is severely constrained by the constituencies they serve and the organizations they fund. For example, the lock-in effect may happen with local funds too in that local governments have great difficulties not continuing to fund a nongovernmental organization once the initial grant is made. Inhibited by local political factors and ignored or defied by local operators, the local governments simply may not be able to do what the federal government wants. Nor are the local constraints only political. Local governments face the same problems with their bureaucrats as does the federal government. The laws of bureaucracy hold here too.

Take the prime sponsors as an example. It is clear that they were the immediate big winners when CETA was enacted in 1973, among other things getting direct power over the distribution of funds that in the past had been distributed by the federal government. These funds, however, were not unrestricted such that the local government could simply figure out what they wanted to do with them and then proceed just as they wished. Rather, these were public funds. Not only that, these monies had a prior history. Pre-CETA funds had gone to various projects, and these projects surely expected to continue as before even if there was a new distribution channel. In short, *to shift power over distribution from federal to local authorities was to shift the target of distributional pressures*.

CETA in essence reshuffled the deck, dealt new hands to redistribute power, and all eyes turned toward the winners. The pressures that were on the old power center were redirected toward the new power point. For the local government prime sponsors, the new setting may have offered a short-lived power trip. Winning power over the distribution of federal funds can carry a fairly high price tag for a prime sponsor.

In a piece of legislation such as CETA, which makes dramatic changes in the distribution of power toward the local level, the federal government, in ways I doubt seriously that it understands, perturbs political, organizational, and bureaucratic forces, sending shock waves throughout the system. The effect goes beyond the local administrative structure and delivery organizations into the broader community in which the delivery mechanism is embedded.

It is much like dropping a stone into a pond with the initial force generating itself out to more distant points. In the pre-CETA days, for example, the Department of Labor negotiated national contracts with organizations such as the Urban League, and local Urban League units simply got the funds to run their programs. CETA eliminated such national contracts, and suddenly the local Urban League project had to fight for its own funds. Local Urban League officials well may have felt less powerful than before as they struggled to convince the local government to keep funding their project. Concomitantly, the local government itself may have felt far from powerful as the Urban League and a host of other manpower projects lined up to tell it how to spend its newfound funds. We will return to this point shortly after getting one other major actor in place.

LOCAL SOCIAL SERVICE DELIVERY ORGANIZATIONS

The local social service delivery organizations and their professional staffs are central to the question of local power—and hence of federal power. In these organizations skilled staff such as teachers or social workers provide services directly to individuals or relatively small groups in a complex setting that is marked by much uncertainty.[17] Elmore has captured the essence of the situation in this statement specifically describing local school systems but pertaining generally to all complex social service delivery programs:

The system is *bottom-heavy* and *loosely-coupled*. It is bottom-heavy because the closer we get to the bottom of the pyramid, the closer we get to the factors that have the greatest effect on the program's success or failure. It is loosely-coupled because the ability of one level to control the behavior of another is weak and largely negative.[18]

---

[17] For an interesting discussion of these organizations, see Paul Berman, *The Study of Macro and Micro Implementation of Social Policy*, The Rand Corporation, P-6071 (January 1978), pp. 24–27.

[18] Richard F. Elmore, *Complexity and Control: What Legislators and Administrators Can Do about Implementation*, Institute of Governmental Research, University of Washington, Public Policy Paper No. 11, April 1979, p. 27, italics in the original.

Increasingly, we are coming to realize the importance of the point of delivery of services and the crucial role of the front line professional staff. These "street-level bureaucrats" include "[teachers], police officers, welfare workers, legal-assistance lawyers, lower-court judges, and health workers. They and other public employees interact with the public and make decisions calling for both individual initiative and considerable routinization."[19] Weatherley and Lipsky observe:

The work of street-level bureaucrats is inherently discretionary. Some influences that might be thought to provide behavioral guidance for them do not actually do much to dictate their behavior. For example, the work objectives for public-service employees are usually vague and contradictory. Moreover, it is difficult to establish or impose valid work-performance measures, and the consumers of services are relatively insignificant as a reference group. Thus street-level bureaucrats are constrained but not directed in their work.

These accommodations and coping mechanisms that they are free to develop form patterns of behavior which become the government program that is "delivered" to the public. In a significant sense, then, street-level bureaucrats *are the policymakers* in their respective work arenas.[20]

The decisions made by front line bureaucrats about which services a client will receive and how the services will be delivered are one of the most powerful determinants of government policy. However, the images conjured up should not be of persons with great power and control themselves. The classroom teacher or the welfare caseworker do not appear as powerful figures, and conversations with them would surely indicate how harried they feel. Yet, when the classroom door closes or the welfare recipient sits down at the caseworker's desk, the unavoidable discretion of the final service deliverers is there.

But it is discretion to deal with a final actor—the treatment recipient—who ultimately has the last word on discretion. That is, the recipient must both be able to benefit from the treatment and

[19]Richard Weatherley and Michael Lipsky, "Street-Level Bureaucrats and Institutional Innovation: Implementing Special-Education Reform," *Harvard Educational Review*, 47 (May 1977), 172.

[20]*Ibid.*, italics in the original.

be willing to receive it. This is vividly illustrated in recent efforts to "upgrade" children's television. As Tom Shales observed in the May 19, 1974 issue of the *Washington Post*: "A sad fact of children's TV reform is that while all the educational consulting and pro-socializing is going on, children still tend to prefer junk when they plop themselves down in front of a TV set. . . . Getting children to like what's good for them—or what some people think is good for them—could well be the hardest job ahead, then, for the children's TV reformers." Shales cites some viewing statistics in which quality shows are pitted directly against the likes of a "Deputy Dawg" cartoon rerun. The outcome was eighty-five percent for junk and fifteen percent for quality. One obvious explanation is that kids want to relax at home and do not want the busman's holiday of more schoollike offerings. The recipients whose welfare is ostensibly the main thrust of a program simply cannot be expected to accept passively what is offered.

It is this final discretion by treatment recipients that makes the discretionary judgments of front line professionals so central to policy. These professionals are the *last* institutional actor. It is their reactions to the treatment recipients' discretionary behavior that is the final institutional link in a long chain of social policy.

The capacity of the front line professionals to make sound judgments in the complex delivery setting—discretionary choices that defy prepackaged answers—is the critical policy input. Their sound judgments over time are the necessary policy ingredient for good programs. This is the positive factor that can make social policies work. Thus, it would be a grave error not to recognize the power—albeit often a negative power to block—at the bottom of the organization. The unavoidable discretion possessed by individuals and/or small units at the point of service delivery may determine what big decisions really look like.

PERCEIVED POWERLESSNESS

As we go from exogenous factors through the street-level bureaucrats, a strong case emerges showing the severe limits of social agency power over desired results. Much of the desired outcome of policy is beyond the direct power of any government. Even where the social agency can influence policy, there are numerous blockages. Expected performance must be cast in terms of the many barriers limiting social agency control which stand between a top-level decision and delivered policy.

The social agency must operate in a setting with a high, un-avoidable level of discretion exerted by nonfederal actors in the field. Moreover, the argument of social agency limits is easily turned to support the limited power of local governments too. The failure to recognize how much unavoidable discretion permeates the management of social service delivery programs can bring great confusion about responsibility and power. And this confusion it-self can further limit power over implementation and performance.

The image that best captures the milieu of social service delivery programs generally and that of shared responsibility for these programs specifically is the perceived powerlessness of the central actors. No matter how many resources a major institutional par-ticipant has, no matter how much relative power an organization has, staff usually feel frustrated, hemmed in, unable to exert dis-cretion. Stepping back from my own field study of CETA and CDBG and other recent work on these programs, I find it is this perception of a lack of power that comes through so vividly.

If we return to the CETA case for an example, perceived power-lessness predominates. DOL staff, particularly in the field, so often seemed to be acting out of pure frustration at their diminished role. A regulatory mentality and harassment were the responses to Congress and the agency hierarchy above who talked as if field staff had "real control" and to grantees who appeared to be cut-ting into the little power they had.

Nor did the big power winners—the prime sponsors—act as if they were masters of the situation. The feds pressed from above; local politicians and organizations suddenly were at the door be-cause the prime sponsors determined the money flow; and below, all of the bureaucratic, organizational, and technical problems of social service delivery programs continued on unrelieved by the granting of more power and discretion to local authorities. *Is it so surprising that innovations did not spring forth, that prime spon-sors so bemoaned the pressures on them rather than racing ahead with new ideas?*

Much the same holds as we move on to the social service delivery organizations, and to street-level bureaucrats. The latter, who scholars keep saying have great amounts of irreducible discretion, perceive themselves as the most powerless organizational actors in the institutional game. They see themselves in a most beleaguered position trapped between regulations and bosses above and difficult clients below.

This pervasive sense of powerlessness is crucial to the development of an agency implementation strategy. Mutual weakness, mutual dependency, and the need for mutual adaptation demand a different style and a different use of resources than one in which either those above or below have great power and act accordingly. The multiplicity of actors and their perceived powerlessness must guide as we turn to agency resources and strategies.

V
Agency Control, Influence, and Responsibility

The last chapter looked broadly at a wide range of forces that can inhibit agency power. The concern now focuses more sharply on the basic issues of the exercise of control or influence and responsibility in large-scale public organizations with many field units.

Control is a fundamental problem in all organizations. Who is to be responsible for it; how is it to be carried out? Consider for a minute the control problems of the social agencies by recasting key elements of the last chapter in more specific organizational terms. A long, hierarchical chain of command characterizes large-scale public organizations (bureaucracies). Political executives must exert control *within the organization* over permanent civil servants who are often distant in terms of bureaucratic layers and/or geography. Moreover, the career staff is likely to have more agency experience and special skills than the political executives. Control within the organization is further complicated "because of the high degree of permeability of the federal agency to outside influence," which means that internal control issues may involve "significant actors in the power setting outside."[1] Dealing with the local governments that deliver services compounds problems for the social agency because of the "weakness of management

---

[1]Donald P. Warwick, *A Theory of Public Bureaucracy: Politics, Personality and Organization in the State Department* (Cambridge, Mass.: Harvard University Presss, 1975), p. 199.

control across jurisdictional boundaries."[2] Here the agency must operate within the broad confines of democratic federalism where each level of government has powers deriving from the Constitution itself and from a long history of past relationships.

The difficulties of management have increased as the social agencies have grown in size and importance. Two sets of issues have emerged. The first concerns responsibility and internal agency control. *Who is to govern these vast public institutions, which have become a permanent part of the American social structure? Who is to keep the agency from the top down oriented toward performance—toward the substantive problems of how to offer better services?* The second set of questions speaks to external control, or more broadly to intergovernmental relations. *What should be the relationship between the federal and local governments where the former has major administrative responsibilities for the program but the latter has responsibility for project operations? How should the social agency manage in this uneasy partnership?*

FEDERAL RESPONSIBILITY FOR PERFORMANCE

Legislative charges to social agencies are likely to be quite detailed with strong language setting out the responsibilities of agency political executives for management in all inclusive terms. For example, the Comprehensive Employment and Training Act was billed as granting localities much greater autonomy and flexibility, yet the legislation charges the secretary with a host of tasks that appear to add up to federal responsibility for *all* performance in the field. The rhetoric of political executive control is embedded clearly in almost all legislation. At the same time the political executives face an almost impossible situation. As Hugh Heclo points out:

. . . to the inherent electoral changes, the American executive political system adds a considerably greater range of nonelectoral uncertainty to

[2]Richard F. Elmore, "Organizational Models of Social Program Implementation," *Public Policy*, 26 (Spring 1978), 198.

political leadership. This system produces top executives who are both expendable over time and in a relatively weak, uncertain position at any one time. . . . without a very steep learning curve, political appointees are likely to find that their capacities for effective action have matured at just about the time they are leaving office. . . . The entire process does not produce long-suffering policymakers who realize their major changes will come gradually through persistence. Most political appointees are more impatient. Any civil servant who offers the standard and often sensible bureaucratic advice to watch, wait, and be careful can expect to arouse more than a little suspicion.[3]

If the chief executive officer and a number of senior vice presidents of business firms came in and went out roughly every two or three years, one must wonder how well their organizations would do. Even if political executives concentrate on program substance, to pursue distant goals that can be accomplished only long after they have left the scene is extremely difficult.

There is another related, complicating dimension in getting the agency moving toward field performance. Legislative language is most explicit that the governance of social programs has as a primary objective managing the delivery of social services so as to increase the benefits accruing from them to program participants. *Performance—if one believes the written word of legislation—is to be the main goal of those who govern.*

In practice, however, that political executives are expected to, or are motivated to see such desired results is far from clear. Instead, the strongest pressures are on maximizing organizational health as indicated by size of staff, dollars appropriated, and the many prerequisites of top-level power. The divergence between organizational health and performance can be large in social service delivery programs funded under grants-in-aid, as this statement by Ingram indicates:

Grant-in-aid programs often place federal agencies in a position where the pursuit of their long-term institutional interests diverges from strict dedication to program implementation. The establishment of a grant program creates powerful forces in a federal agency's political environment. States

---

[3]Hugh Heclo, *A Government of Strangers: Executive Politics in Washington* (Washington, D.C.: The Brookings Institution, 1977), p. 110.

become the clientele of the agency, and the better they can be served, the more credit comes to the agency. Consequently, it should be no surprise when federal agencies place the highest priority upon achieving constituency approval in allocating grant funds. The tendency of federal granting agencies is to pursue grant allocation practices that gain broad support, even if this means refusing to terminate funds for reasons of noncompliance or poor performance, or failing to reward states that excel in program objectives.[4]

High-level, short-term political executives find themselves more and more concerned with preserving organizational health and comfort. And here they worry first about top-level relationships and second about the problems in the field which can explode into crises at the top. The crises that need managing usually arise from fraud or dishonesty, poor treatment of someone who has access to a political figure, and failures to carry out distributional decisions about which group or area is to receive funds (how the pie is cut); not from problems of poor organizational or program performance. Organizational health or political expedience often weigh more heavily on the political executives than substantive programmatic concerns.

Let me reinforce this absolutely critical point of the dominance of other issues over performance with some examples from CETA and CDBG. The latter has been a continuing battle royal among cities and between cities and suburbs from its inception in the Nixon administration through President Carter's effort to hold down federal spending to fight inflation. The earlier struggles were primarily between big cities and powerful urban counties. The urban counties were left out by much of the Great Society legislation which targeted funds on the poverty areas of central cities or the depressed rural counties. The biggest early fight in CDBG was for the urban counties to get their share. Now the hot issue of distribution is in terms of geographic regions. A *Washington Post* headline of November 27, 1978 that reads "Sun Belt and Frost Belt Cities War over Waning Federal Aid" captures the essence of the latest distributional fight. *Indeed, the politics of dis-*

---

[4]Helen Ingram, "Policy Implementation through Bargaining: The Case of Federal Grants-in-Aid," *Public Policy*, 25 (Fall 1977), 525.

tribution is the longest running game in town. Nothing can turn legislators to action so fast as a threat to the flow of funds to their district or state.

Running close, however, is scandal or fraud in a public program. CETA had it all in the summer of 1978. On the sensational side, there were allegations of CETA funds buying sexual favors. Less juicy, but more prevalent, were CETA jobs going to relatively well-to-do persons with political connections. The *Washington Post* saw fit to publish the value of one CETA employee's home and went so far as to carry a picture of the house with the story.

Performance issues such as job placement problems of CETA persons after they leave the CETA job and the low levels of expenditures by local governments on training to prepare CETA people for private industry jobs do make it into newspaper print on occasion. But this seems to happen *only* when there is an in-depth story of CETA issues, and then performance problems get tucked away in the article after the items of scandal and fraud or distribution have been discussed.

Political executives should answer for play in *both* the organizational health and performance games. But this is difficult because to do so requires doing battle on two widely separate fronts with different demands and starkly different time frames.

Good organizational health becomes the first order of business for the agency because the threats to it are highly visible with the potential for immediate disaster in Washington. The obvious justification is that the agency cannot carry out its basic program mission if it is in political trouble. But staying out of trouble often demands constant attention that takes resources from the performance game. More insidiously, organizational health may determine the saliency of issues even when the agency looks toward the field. Issues of *compliance* such as fraud and distributional directives, not *performance*, predominate because these are areas of political volatility.

The performance game involves a long, slow buildup of agency resources where achievements are hard to measure and usually long in coming. *And there may be the ultimate irony in the very nature of social service delivery programs themselves: The inherent complexity that makes detection of poor performance so dif-*

ficult and progress so slow adds up to less pressure to do well and less danger of explosive events that shatter the agency. There will still be commitment to the performance game. But a continuing, extended commitment to improve performance is hard to sustain, and often loses out at the margin to issues of organizational health.

We can rail at Congress or the agencies but the basic problem remains of getting a sustained effort toward performance. The rewards and punishments in the federal system simply do not demand such a commitment. Nothing forces the implementation perspective. It is the other way around in terms of the dynamics of federal policy—factors push up, away from a focus on performance in the field. Responsibility for performance in general and implementation specifically is an unsettled and unsettling issue in federal agencies.

CONTROL AND DECENTRALIZATION

After responsibility comes the issue of agency control. As Anthony and Dearden observe: "*A business company, or indeed any organization, must be controlled; that is, there must be devices that insure that it goes where its leaders want it to go.*"[5] In large-scale organizations, hierarchical control involves a complex process whereby those at the top must induce intermediate level managers to behave so as to lead others to respond as desired.

Control in large-scale organizations almost never fits the old military image of command with an unquestioned response to an order. As Anthony has pointed out: "The word control in its ordinary sense has unfortunate connotations. . . . It often is used in the sense of 'boss, curb, dominate, enforce, forestall, hinder, inhibit, manipulate, prevail, restrain, shackle, and watch,' and these connotations are not at all realistic as descriptions of what actually goes on in a well-managed organization."[6] Management control ultimately comes down to the intangible ability of top managers to

---

[5]Robert N. Anthony and John Dearden, *Management Control Systems: Text and Cases*, (Homewood, Ill.: 3d ed. Richard D. Irwin 1976), p. 3.

[6]Robert N. Anthony, *Planning and Control Systems* (Cambridge, Mass.: Harvard University Press, 1965), p. 28.

motivate line managers to motivate others. "Psychological considerations are dominant in management control. Activities such as communicating, persuading, exhorting, inspiring, and criticizing are an important part of the process."[7]

When top decision makers are located at headquarters and most of the implementers and the operators are in the field, the key question is how much discretion should headquarters grant. To have centralized authority or not, that is the question. As Lundquist observes: ". . . decentralization is a general problem of organizations. In all the meanings in which the term is used, there is a common denominator, namely, 'away from the centre.' "[8]

A critical device for supporting more decentralized management is a formal control system. Anthony and Dearden define such a system as follows:

A control system is a system whose purpose is to maintain a desired state or condition. Any control system has at least these four elements:

1. A measuring device which detects what is happening in the parameter being controlled, that is, a detector.

2. A device for assessing the significance of what is happening, usually by comparing information of what *is actually happening* with some standard of expectation of what *should be happening*, that is, a selector.

3. A device for altering behavior if the need for doing so is indicated, that is, an effector.

4. A means for communicating information among these devices.[9]

The basic requirements for more decentralized control appear to be (1) objectives and standards for which there are measurable control points and appropriate measuring mechanisms in place; (2) clear, enforceable sanctions that guide performance, inhibit the overstepping of boundaries, or preferably both; and (3) good means

[7]Robert N. Anthony, John Dearden, and Richard F. Vancil, *Management Control Systems: Text and Cases* (Homewood, Ill.: Richard D. Irwin, 1972), p. 5.

[8]Lennart Lundquist, *Means and Goals of Political Decentralization*, Malmö, Sweden: Studentlitteratur, 1972), p. 13.

[9]*Management Control Systems*, 3rd ed., pp. 3–4, italics in the original.

of communicating what is desired or proscribed. That is, the organization needs to be able to communicate measurable boundaries and sanctions and to apply those sanctions to reward (e.g., managers' salaries based on profits) or to punish in terms of the boundaries.

FROM CONTROL TO INFLUENCE

Decentralization is a common problem for large-scale organizations whether in the public or private sector. Just as do corporate managers, political executives must decide how much discretion to grant explicitly to subordinate units including their (regional office) field staffs. But there is also a fundamental difference. In the business area top management will be able at least to some degree to choose between decentralization and centralization in the traditional sense of having direct organizational authority over *all* implementers and operators. It only has to confront a *within* organization choice. But Congress in effect rules out such direct authority by opting for shared governance between political jurisdictions. When the social agency considers the question of tight control versus decentralization for its own field staff, it is a second-order decision made *after* the political one that puts project operators within the jurisdiction of another political entity.

This last point is critical. *A number of the key implementers and all those who run projects operate outside of the traditional within-organizational control devices.* However, even though these people are in other organizations and often in other political jurisdictions, social legislation so often fixes the top political executives responsibility for operations as if *all* administrative units and service deliverers were segments of a single organization. The rhetoric of hierarchical (within) organization control is there. It is not a very useful way of thinking about how social agencies "control" implementation and operations.

Let us look at the implementation issue from the other side. As Lundquist proposes:

If the angle of approach is changed to that of the implementer, one can formulate the problem by posing the question: why does the implementer obey the decision maker's steering [direction]? For the large organization, which is involved here, at least three sets of reasons can be imagined:

(1) the implementer obeys for fear of penalty or wish for reward.

(2) the implementer obeys because he believes the decision to be rational or because it agrees with his evaluations.

(3) the implementer obeys because he appreciates the decision maker personally or because he always obeys the steering communications from certain organization roles, irrespective of who occupies the role.[10]

The first response fits well the image of strict hierarchy with the implementer motivated by clear sanctions either of force or positive and negative inducements (promotion, higher pay). The third response is either to charismatic authority or to traditional or legal authority. In modern large-scale organizations the latter is more likely and also fits the hierarchical structure. The remaining response flows from what Lundquist labels "expert power," and which I call "credibility." It is quite different from the other two: not a response to a command, an authority figure, or to direct sanctions, but to a recommendation or to advice. There is a clear choice: implement as prescribed if the prescription makes sense. There is the further implication that the notion makes sense, especially in highly ambiguous areas, because the recommender has a reasonably good track record. Credibility is earned; authority comes from direct force or granted status. The latter is control in the traditional sense; the former seems more aptly described as influence.

BARGAINING AND FIXING

Influence more and more is the name of the game. Daniel Elazar has written that "It may not be too great an exaggeration to suggest that the historical model that most closely resembles the federal government in its domestic role today is the Holy Roman Empire

---

[10]Lundquist, p. 36. The steering definition is found at p. 27 and the concept discussed at pp. 33–37. Note: He defines steering as "the decision maker's conscious attempts to influence the implementation in a certain direction."

in those periods where the Emperor's domestic powers were contingent on the cooperation of his barons."[11]

Bargaining becomes the appropriate strategy where the power of hierarchical control in the traditional sense ends, where the credible threat of command and control with clear sanctions that apply to discernible boundary points no longer holds. In the social agency top managers cannot rely solely on the power of hierarchy to induce lower level managers in their *own* field organizations to do their bidding. However, there is still the distinct advantage of being in a superior position. At the bargaining table with local governments, the social agency is at best an equal in the negotiations. There is no trump card of direct hierarchical authority to play. The guide to play needs to be cast in a bargaining mode where power is defined in terms of directional influence, not direct command.

Good bargaining strategy requires a search for leverage points—those places where the bargainer's involvement is likely to yield a high return because he has a scarce resource the other party wants. For example, if an individual owns a key parcel of land that is critical to a proposed shopping center, the owner may demand ten or fifteen percent of the total payment for the land even though he has only five percent of the acreage.

Leverage derives from positional advantage. Leveraging makes sense only when two or more parties perceive gains from bargaining and hence would be willing to move in the desired direction. It is good horse trading at the margin where there is a willing buyer and seller.

Leveraging becomes particularly important where there is no brute power to force desired behavior. Those who can command an action be taken and insure its execution with the threat of strong sanctions need not bother with either the hard search for potential leverage points or the subtle moves to secure the bargain. Those with strong direct *control* do not have to scurry about for positional advantage where a relatively weak push may tip the scale. Such luxury, it must be clear, is not possessed by the social agency in

---

[11] Daniel J. Elazar, "The Problem of Political Distance," *National Civic Review*, 67 (July 1978), 338.

the performance game. As Ingram has pointed out in her discussion of federal grants-in-aid to states:

As a result of grant bargaining, federal administrative agencies can facilitate change in a willing state. But in the absence of state commitment, the federal agency cannot compel state policy change. The federal government is at best a peripheral participant in the state political process.[12]

To leverage, the player must not only find a positional advantage but have flexible resources to put up at the leverage point. Money may be the most flexible resource; yet technical aid or organizational power such as granting a rule variation may be more useful. However, all such resources need to be discretionary. As discussed earlier, the provision of federal funds to nonfederal organizations for continuing activities locks funds in by creating a reverse presumption (the funder-provider must "prove" the case for withdrawal). The agency needs to be able to come to the bargaining table with uncommitted resources in its pocket.

Fixing presents another set of institutional problems. Fixing, of course, is always happening—usually willy-nilly as things break down. The problem is to get fixing established near enough to the top so it can have direction and leadership.

In *The Implementation Game*, Bardach found a fixer in Assemblyman Frank Lanterman of California whose extended efforts over time shaped the implementation of the Lanterman-Petris-Short (L-P-S) Act of 1967, legislation termed "the Magna Carta" of the mentally ill. Lanterman was the senior Republican on the powerful Ways and Means Committee. He was coming to the end of his career and considered the L-P-S Act as the capstone of his work in mental health. " . . . mental health policy," as Bardach points out, "was Lanterman's territory and . . . no significant changes in that area could be made without his consent or, alternatively, without having him exact a price."[13]

Lanterman was the architect of the direction the L-P-S Act was to go, had power to intervene, and was willing to take the time to

---

[12]Ingram, p. 521, italics in the original.
[13]Eugene Bardach, *The Implementation Game* (Cambridge, Mass.: The MIT Press, 1977), p. 13. See pp. 9–35 for the account of Lanterman in action.

work through adjustments along the way. Here was the fixer par excellence. He was in the pivotal position with the commitment and the capability to make on-the-spot adjustments in the dynamics of play.

But position alone is not enough. A fixer needs all kinds of help. As Bardach indicated in discussing Lanterman's role:

Is all this to say that only "power" counts when it comes to fixing the implementation game? Not at all. Formal authority and formal political resources count for much but not for everything. The fixer must be able to intervene effectively, but he or she must be able to know where, when, and about what. To know these things, he or she must have access to a great deal of information and have the flow of information summarized, interpreted, and validated so that he or she can make sense of it. . . . Just as money attracts money, information attracts information. Without information about how implementation games were being played "out there" in the field, Lanterman would have been powerless to do any fixing.[14]

The fixer must operate with an underlying base of technical and organizational resources. The institutional structure must provide needed information, and the analysis of that information must support new strategies and tactics by the fixer over time.

Fixing may be the most difficult of tasks. Bardach has captured its essence when he observed:

Game-fixing is quintessentially government by men rather than laws. It is not necessarily, though, irresponsible government. . . .

The real problem . . . is that too few of the would-be fixers know how to do the right thing, are willing to do it if they do know how, and have the political resources to make their will effective. The most problematic role in the fixer coalition, the one that is hardest to come by, is the intervener at the top, the person or persons with powerful political resources.[15]

Generally, bargaining and fixing together are the preferred mode of play in the performance game. In the dynamics of play, bargaining and fixing blend together. Through negotiating or repair-

---

[14]*Ibid.*, pp. 277–278. See pp. 268–284 for a discussion of fixing the implementation game.
[15]*Ibid.*, p. 279.

ing, or renegotiating after repairs, the agency may be able to influence local organizations to move toward better organizational and program performance.

INDIRECT CONTROLS: THE SEARCH FOR MARKETLIKE FORCES

One of the most troubling aspects of federal funding is this lack of pressure points pushing the social agencies and the organizations they fund toward better performance in the field. The situation has led many people to argue that government's unresponsiveness to performance means we had better turn to the play of the market.[16] In setting out a number of "postliberal heresies," Bardach puts the case against government most forcefully:

A second heresy has asserted that even when we know what ought to be done, and can get political leaders to agree to mandate it, government is probably ill suited to do the job. At the very least, it is likely that the bureaucratic and regulatory strategies government has traditionally relied upon are ineffective if not mischievous. Economists, both liberal and conservative, have taken the lead here and have argued persuasively that manipulating the marketplace may often be a better strategy than trying to abolish it or inventing a substitute for it.[17]

The claim is that Adam Smith's unseen hand or the workings of supply and demand—that is, competition with far less government involvement—will make for greater efficiency and effectiveness in government policies. Hence, we need to consider the extent to which marketlike forces (or what can be called indirect controls) can generate pressures for improving performance either within organizations or external to them.

---

[16]The need to rely upon market forces in the public sector has been espoused by a number of individuals—the most useful general treatments being by Charles Schultze and Robert Levine. Schultze has made his argument over a number of years with the most recent statement being Charles L. Schultze, *The Public Use of Private Interest* (Washington, D.C.: The Brookings Institution, 1977). Levine's most extended treatment is presented in Robert A. Levine, *Public Planning: Failure and Redirection* (New York: Basic Books, 1972).

[17]Bardach, *The Implementation Game*, p. 4.

The market model, however, only works well under rather restrictive conditions. As Richard Nelson observes: "It must be recognized . . . that the great efficacy alleged from marketlike organization rests on two empirical propositions. One is that the market-failure problems are not very serious in most sectors; second, that the remedies for these problems often are easy to apply and effective."[18] Moreover, the market model is most likely to break down in the complex service areas that we are considering:

The conventional wisdom is that no one knows self-interests better than the person or group affected, but there are serious reasons to doubt that this holds in all cases. . . . Many parents know little about what goes on in the school their children are attending, and have little information and knowledge on which to judge alternatives; clearly, parental choice cannot bear the full weight of the decision mechanism. Indeed, in a large number of problem sectors there is reason to doubt that consumers or voters have enough knowledge to make good choices. . . .

Nor does reliance on for-profit enterprise seem a general solution to the problem of supply organization. The case for for-profit supply is strong where the good or service in question is easily evaluated by consumers, and where there is considerable competition among suppliers. Where these conditions do not hold, there is good reason to adopt regimes of supply organization that can internalize, to some extent, the demanders' interest— governmental or not-for-profit forms, or other mechanisms of public control that damp or channel the profit motive.[19]

An example of a market arrangement to provide social services will show both the potential and the problems. The example I'll use is a payment voucher to go *directly* to a person eligible for training under a program such as CETA. The recipient of the voucher would then have resources to "buy" employment training either from a teaching institution such as a community college or from an employer. In the latter case the voucher would be used as

[18]Richard R. Nelson, *The Moon and the Ghetto: An Essay on Public Policy Analysis* (New York: W. W. Norton & Co., 1977), pp. 46–47. Nelson goes on to point out at p. 47: "If political scientists can be accused of seeing the hand of formal government everywhere, and the need for it almost everywhere, the economists can be accused of arguing away the need for government almost anywhere, and advocating the almost universal superiority of the hidden hands of consumer sovereignty and competition among suppliers to meet consumer demands."
[19]*Ibid.*, pp. 48–49.

a form of wage subsidy to the employer to cover costs of training on the job. The voucher by coming directly to trainees would permit them to search through alternative training opportunities. They would not be restricted to the limited opportunities offered by established CETA projects. Rather there would be the working of the marketplace with many buyers and sellers. Institutions offering classroom training or on-the-job training would compete for clients by pushing toward better services, lower prices, or both.

Under the voucher plan, however, some level of government would have to be involved. At a minimum, government would determine or regulate the determination of eligibility for a voucher probably based on income level and employment status. There also could be efforts to regulate what training is offered although the danger exists that this might be perceived as too much government interference. So eligibility determination could be the only additional government activity beyond already existing regulation of suppliers (e.g., existing state and federal laws pertaining to educational institutions). There could be an opportunity for the promised efficiencies and benefits of private market forces to accrue.

We still may not obtain the results that are desired, however. The efficient and effective training techniques that have eluded government thus far well may elude those offering services in the marketplace. The "law of markets" does not guarantee technical breakthroughs or yield an automatic solution to the immense organizational problems that bedevil complex social service delivery programs. In short, there is no guarantee of much higher performance. The potential benefits of marketlike forces must be cast in realistic terms.

There is another problem. It is the basic political question of government's willingness to stop in the face of less than desired outcomes. What happens if schools "sell" training that does not yield jobs, or businesses let people go after the wage subsidy period? Do politicians and interest groups say philosophically, and perhaps quite realistically, government has done all it can in providing the basic opportunity through financial support to get needed training? Do they say this even though large numbers of participants do not benefit as they and we hoped, and even though the nation does not gain the increased productive power that also was desired? As Schultze warns:

> Because incentive-oriented approaches to social intervention rely on decentralized reactions to prices, they seem to deprive government of control of case-by-case results. If nothing else, this would make legislators nervous. They would have to forgo the opportunity to provide their programs with all sorts of adjudication procedures drawn up to take care of specific losses. They would also forfeit the opportunity to second-guess administrators and to provide services for constituents through intervention in administrative decisions.[20]

Going the market route does not escape organizational and political issues that are at the heart of social policy. The temptation is for government to do more, to intervene more forcefully. However, Schultze's further warning should be heeded: " . . . in all cases the comparison should be between an imperfect market and an imperfect [government] regulatory scheme, not some ideal abstraction."[21]

Where does this leave us? As usual no sure path opens up without dangers. One obvious problem is not to be trapped by the lure of the market as a panacea. It will not let us off the hook anymore than passing responsibilities to local governments will. That point should be clear before there are any leaps to the free market bandwagon with vouchers or direct payments to industry. At the same time it does appear desirable to seek marketlike pressures that operate indirectly as goads to better performance *at least as a supplement to direct influence efforts*. The difficulty is in finding ones that make technical, bureaucratic, and political sense.

---

[20]Schultze, *The Public Use of Private Interest*, p. 72.
[21]*Ibid.*, p. 38.

VI
Organizational Resources

Agency resources are the final factor to be considered before turning in the next chapter to the task of building an agency implementation strategy. What resources are available to the agency to inform, induce, and help local administrative and operating (service delivery) organizations carry out what is intended? Sequentially, the first issue is whether the social agency has the resources to get a commitment from the local organization. But the ultimate issue is whether the two partners together can muster enough resources for effective service delivery at the local level. The local organization must be not only willing, but able, to deliver services. To do that it is likely to require lots of help, including an effort extending over a considerable period of time to raise capacity.

INFORMATION

Information is the raw material of governance generally, and of implementation specifically. Can the agency both develop good information and get it to the people who need it for decisions and implementation? At issue are both the technical means available to produce sound information (the limits of methodology) and the political/bureaucratic question of access. Because of the complexity of its development, information will require considerable discussion.

Information will be employed in the common dictionary sense of that which informs. It can be highly technical. Information may

82   *Organizational Resources*

show the specifications of a complex scientific process. Or, information may have been developed through complex procedures
such as large-scale surveys indicating socioeconomic conditions.
But it need not be. That the chairman of an agency's appropriations
subcommittee would not stand for a project in his district being
defunded clearly is not science-based information, but it surely is
vital and policy relevant. All sorts of information having to do
with social, economic, political, and bureaucratic phenomena may
be useful for policy purposes.

In terms of the policy process we can distinguish the following
information uses: *policy or decision formulation, control, and
advice.* Policy formulation is a continuing effort to determine in
relatively broad terms an organization's future policy directions
and how to pursue them. Given our notions that much of policy is
determined at the operational level, the better name for this activity
may be decision formulation, but we'll stick with the standard
usage of policy formulation. Control and advice are more specific,
more detailed in speaking to particular aspects of carrying out of
policies (decisions) once formulated. Control, as we have discussed, involves efforts by an organization or a unit of an organization to *direct* the activities of other organizations or units. In the
case of a social agency directions to grantees for which it has
administrative responsibilities may indicate (1) target groups to be
served, (2) administrative, organizational, or programmatic approaches and procedures to follow, and (3) expected organizational
and programmatic *performance* levels.[1] Advice is focused on the
same general areas as control offering specific means of complying
with directives or reaching performance levels. But advice, including extended support such as for capacity building, is proffered on
a take it or leave it basis. Control gives directives to be in compliance with guidelines or reach performance standards; advice
speaks to means of compliance or performance but with the intent
that choice rests with the recipient of the advice to follow a suggested approach or to accept proposed resources such as training.

---

[1]The distinction between organizational and programmatic performance will be
made clear shortly.

Definitions

At this point we need to lay out some definitions that are central to a discussion of information uses both specifically in implementation and more generally in the areas of control, advice, and policy formulation. Most of the concern in this section is with organizational or programmatic information classified under three headings: inputs, outputs, and outcomes.

Inputs are the elements (e.g., a particular training manual) or physical arrangements (an intake desk that applicants are to come to before being assigned to a job counselor) in a project or program. Outputs describe organizational behavior by staff members in servicing clients and administering the organization as an institution. Inputs are the static factors or components that sum up to the "on paper" description of an activity. As such, inputs can be verified without extended observation or qualitative judgments. The analogy is a checklist. Outputs are different in having a dynamic quality that must be observed or judged over time. For example, a look at records or brief observation can determine that a teacher has certain educational qualifications or is utilizing specified teaching materials, but only by observing the person in action can we determine how these various inputs actually are being used in providing services.

Outcomes define benefits to the recipients of service. At issue is whether participants are better off after receiving a service. It is useful to distinguish distributional, proximate, and final outcomes. Distributional outcomes show the target groups (e.g., blacks, the aged, or the poor) or geographic areas that receive funds and/or services. They say who got what tangible things, such as funds, training, etc. Final outcomes speak to whether a program or project has improved the long-run status of the participants—for example, whether the individuals in training or education projects have experienced significant positive changes in their capacities to earn or to learn. Final outcomes may be determinable only in the distant future, so it may be necessary to obtain proximate outcomes that indicate intermediate results expected to lead toward desired final outcomes. If a training project in welding has an expected final outcome of increased earnings over time, proximate outcomes might include obtaining a job after training, getting a job in welding or a related speciality, or holding a job for six consecutive months after training. Positive results do not show conclusively that a participant has improved his or her long-run earning capability. However, their presence does suggest that individuals are moving in the right direction. *Their absence (e.g., no job or working in an unskilled position after specialized training) indicates even more strongly that participants are not moving toward longer run benefits.*

We can now distinguish between organizational and program performance. How resources are employed (how the staff uses inputs and behaves) is what I've called organizational performance. What happens to program or project participants is deemed program performance. When we ask how well a program or project is working, we are addressing the basic issues of organizational and program performance.

These elements of performance can be thought of in terms of a "theory" about program delivery. When a law is passed, the ostensible assumption is that program inputs and outputs (organizational performance) will produce desired objectives (program performance). For example, the explicit (or at least implicit) theory in elementary and secondary school legislation is that if certain school materials (inputs) are used in the prescribed way (outputs), children in the classroom will learn more (outcomes). In essence there is a hypothesis about cause and effect. However complex the social policy setting, we should not lose sight of the fact that what is at issue is whether the use of human and other resources (inputs and behavior) will bring a desired outcome.

A Basic Distinction in Information Needs

A critical, and fundamental, distinction can be made between information for exercising control and information for offering advice or formulating policy. Pinpointing noncompliance and poor organizational or program performance in such a way as to support control requires hard, specific data. Advice in particular, but also policy formulation, can draw on "softer, richer" information including that showing how organizational processes and procedures are used in the political/bureaucratic environment in the provision of social services.

The exercise of control demands evidence sufficiently specific and precise to support the claim of wrongdoing against a funded organization. The need is for an underlying empirical base in which inputs, outputs, and outcomes are defined in measurable terms that are not subject to significant controversy and are measured with a relatively high degree of accuracy. Conversely, the more a particular measure is challengeable either as to whether it represents the desired result (i.e., are wages immediately after training a good indicator of long-term earnings changes?) or on statistical grounds, the weaker is the empirical base of control.[2]

The provision of advice establishes different demands. The lack of proven approaches that characterizes social service delivery programs places a real premium on information drawn from extensive field experience. The scarce commodity is organizational and programmatic experience that can aid in seeing and *sensing* where something is wrong. Often the most useful, and the only available, information on which to base such advice comes from "having been there before." Such information is likely to come from the competent bureaucratic professional who has lived through past organizational and program difficulties, rather than from the organizational theorist.

I have made the basic distinction concerning information demands by using the loaded terms of "hard, specific" and "softer, richer." While these are intended to convey a needed impression, they also oversimplify the situation and hence can be misleading. The crucial distinction reflects the uses to which the information is to be put, not the information's statistical qualities, even though generally a stronger empirical case must be made to *force* a change on a reluctant organization than to provide ideas on how to attack a perceived problem or to formulate broad policies. This distinction must be elaborated on in this chapter to make its meaning more

---

[2]In statistical jargon, the challenges would be to the validity and reliability of the measure.

clear, but I emphasize at this point that the distinction in what information is required for different purposes is central to devising a reasonable information strategy.

THE ART AND SCIENCE OF INFORMATION DEVELOPMENT

This section will consider the present technical capability for developing field information to be used in policy formulation, control, and advice. Most of the discussion will focus on the underlying capability of available information techniques to generate sufficiently sound information on organizational and programmatic performance to exercise control. From this base, however, we can also discuss the information needed to support the provision of advice and the formulation of policy.

The Weakness of Final-Outcome Evaluations for Supporting Federal Control

The big question of social policy has been "Does it work?" as measured by benefits to program and project participants. It was in the social programs that people first began calling seriously for final-outcome evaluations of existing programs, more particularly the Great Society programs. And the demand was for hard-nosed, science-based field investigations capable of providing *definitive* empirical evidence about a policy's effectiveness in improving social conditions.[3]

Hard data on whether programs and projects worked were to be the foundation of hierarchical control. Complications arising from the interactions of theory, methodology, politics, institutions, and people, however, have severely limited the direct usefulness of these results for control in social agency management. Although no

---

[3]Recommendations for final-outcome evaluations and the expectations about payoffs can be found in numerous places. Two of the most influential were Joseph S. Wholey and others, *Federal Evaluation Policy* (Washington, D.C.: Urban Institute, 1970); and Alice M. Rivlin, *Systematic Thinking for Social Action* (Washington, D.C.: The Brookings Institution, 1971).

relatively short discussion will do justice to the complex issue of whether final-outcome evaluations can provide information of sufficient accuracy and timeliness to support the federal control of locally operated and administered social service delivery programs, let us consider briefly in nontechnical terms some of the problems of doing such studies.

The biggest problem is the nature of social service programs themselves. Social problems are complex and hard to treat. Realistically, the outcome effects are likely to be small. Yet new social programs get cast in soaring rhetoric with vague objectives but alluring promises of success. This presents a formidable challenge to technique, as Rossi and Wright point out:

. . . demonstrated effects of the [social program] intervention will usually be weaker than proponents originally hoped or promised . . . [so] evaluation methodology must be sensitive or powerful enough to detect small effects. . . .

The combination of vaguely defined goals, deeply rooted and recalcitrant social problems, high expectations, and weak effects ideally requires robust methodology and powerful designs.[4]

But it has proven most difficult to find methods sufficiently robust and designs sufficiently powerful to handle the complexity of social service programs and yield sound outcome results. As I have observed:

. . . it is a near certainty that a competent methodologist can call into question such things as the test used, the drawing of the sample, the comparability of the control group. In short, no evaluation can be expected to be unassailable in terms of its methodological and field development. And these deficiencies open up the debate so that ideological or political concerns can be pursued in a methodological framework.[5]

---

[4]Peter H. Rossi and Sonia R. Wright, "Evaluation Research: An Assessment of Theory, Practice, and Politics," *Evaluation Quarterly,* 1 (February 1977), 10. This is an excellent review article for readers interested in more details on evaluation research.

[5]Walter Williams, *Social Policy Research and Analysis: The Experience in the Federal Social Agencies* (New York: Elsevier, 1971), p. 104. There is another,

Limited evaluative techniques can be overwhelmed by internal bureaucratic factors and external realities. Both politicians and bureaucrats may employ the technical limitations in final-outcome results to avoid making decisions. Difficult political choices can be postponed indefinitely on the basis of need for further, more authoritative (read politically incontestable) information.

These technical, bureaucratic, and political problems do not rule out the use of final-outcome evaluations. However, it is far from clear that such evaluations at this time provide much of a basis for social agency control over projects that are administered and operated by local governments or other nonfederal entities. *These severe limits on the usefulness of final-outcome evaluations to support from above have profound implications for social agency structure and function.*

Distributional and Proximate Outcomes

Distributional and proximate outcomes often may be determined through quite straightforward methods. If the distributional goal is an easily defined and ascertained factor, such as race, ethnicity, age, or sex, the basic requirement is for simple head counting. If the measurement problem is more difficult, such as determining yearly income to see if persons are poor, methodological complexity will increase along with the cost of getting information. Much the same can be said about proximate outcomes. Employment, length of employment, wage rates, hours of work per week, and similar factors can be measured with a relatively high degree of accuracy by trained interviewers. For a welding program to train Vietnam veterans, hard data can show whether a former trainee was a veteran and is holding a welding job. And the results that a

---

perhaps even more complex, problem of measurement. The effect of projects such as those aimed at training may not be measurable in terms of specific participants at a point in time but only in terms of broad labor market changes over time. While such an issue is beyond the scope of this work, its implications reinforce what is being said here about the difficulty of measurement. For a discussion of this measurement issue, see Henry J. Aaron, *Politics and the Professors* (Washington, D.C.: The Brookings Institution, 1978), pp. 125–138.

veteran has such a job do indicate that the first big step has been made.[6]

Distributional and proximate outcome measures are more modest in intent than those for final outcomes in not being expected to show that projects are yielding lasting benefits for participants. These intermediate measures, however, can indicate the extent to which projects are complying with legislative and agency demands. Since present methodological tools can be used to assess these intermediate outcomes with a reasonably high degree of accuracy, *distributional and proximate outcomes may provide stronger levers of control than the more controversial final outcomes.*

Implementation Assessments

Implementation assessment is the label given to research-oriented efforts to investigate organizational performance (inputs and outputs).[7] Such studies as the name implies concentrate on the process by which organizations (usually large-scale ones) move from a decision to start a new program or modify an existing one to the point of having that change (innovation) fully in place—that is, fully operational.

In these assessments the major emphasis is on how people behave in their organizational status or role. Such behavior is shaped both by the internal resources and structure of the institution and by the external demands of the environment upon that institution. Of importance are four overlapping but distinct kinds of dynamic behavior: (1) what organizational staff members do with nonhuman resources (inputs), such as programmatic elements and internal organizational arrangements; (2) how staff members behave with

---

[6]The reader knowledgeable about statistics will realize that we cannot say definitively that the training helped produce the job unless we have a comparison base (untrained veterans) to determine the extent to which veterans get welding jobs without training.

[7]For a more detailed discussion of the notion of implementation assessment, see Walter Williams, "Implementation Analysis and Assessment," in *Social Program Implementation,* ed. Walter Williams and Richard F. Elmore (New York: Academic Press, 1976), pp. 267–292, esp. pp. 282–286.

each other; (3) how they behave with staff members of other organizations with which their organization must interact in its external environment; and (4) what they do in treating those who are expected to benefit from their services.

The critical feature of these studies is their capacity to provide rich detail about both an organization's history and procedures, and the four kinds of dynamic staff behavior listed earlier. Through careful observation and questioning one can assess how much confusion, lack of clarity, or outright contradiction exist in terms of desired organizational behavior; how administrative duties are executed; how staff delivers services; and what happens in the decision-making process, including the extent to which clients and other citizens have a real say.

Available techniques may yield strong evidence that a project is making no effort to do what is desired or is fouling up that effort. The evidence may be sufficiently sound to support the exercise of control at least to the extent of indicating clear losers. The greatest potential for improving agency governance, however, is likely to come from softer, richer data that can expand the empirical base for providing advice and formulating policy.

Care must be taken not to oversell what can be done. There can be major problems. First implementation assessments, just as evaluations, require measurable criteria if there is to be a judgment about success. Second, the precise measurement of complex organizational behavior is difficult. Clearly the results are often subject to challenge. Despite these caveats, I think useful decision-making information can be gathered from observation and interviews indicating in detail the extent to which an organization is trying to do what is desired. As I have observed elsewhere:

. . . people with well-honed bureaucratic sensitivities should be able to assess within tolerable limits how well an activity is going and whether it is beginning to fit into its institutional environment. Surely it ought to be possible to spot the bad cases—but not necessary to know what to do about them, since that step requires ex ante prediction.

The central role of reasoned judgment in assessing implementation should be clearly delineated. A static checklist of all the specified inputs (one teacher, two teacher aides, three talking typewriters, and so on) will not indicate the viability of the project. On the other hand, enough missing pieces may spell trouble. The exercise of judgment or of a composite of judgments of an activity in motion seems the only way to determine viability. At the same time, technique may facilitate judgment. A set of "dynamic" questions (e.g., does the principal support the project?), a common scaling system, or a sampling frame may keep those carrying out the assessment from missing important issues, provide a useful means of comparing judgments, and avoid selectivity biases. Good judgment, however, remains the key element. Methodology simply does not appear to be the big barrier. Nor do I see the need for highly trained social scientists to carry out the various tasks. The biggest need is for competent, reasonable people with sound substantive knowledge of programs and of bureaucracy.[8]

Implications of the Information Deficiencies

Let me quickly tie together the present critique of information capabilities with the earlier discussion of control and influence. The previous two chapters indicated how limited was the ability of social agencies to exercise direct control because of political and bureaucratic factors. *In particular, grants-in-aid that provide operating funds to another political jurisdiction but charge the federal agency with management responsibilities make that uneasy partnership more amenable to influence than control.*

The difficulties of obtaining sound data add another barrier to the exercise of management control. In Anthony and Dearden's terms, the agency lacks strong "detectors." And nowhere is this more critical than in the case of final outcomes. Woefully weak are available tools for asking if programs are working in the sense of yielding long-term benefits. Greater capacity is available to assess distributional and proximate outcomes and organizational performance. But even here technical weaknesses combined with difficulties of using sanctions hardly make a solid base of control.

The agency has much more opportunity to exert influence through advice and policy formulation, through bargaining and fixing. And here the softer, richer data of implementation assessment can be crucial. Shortly, we will turn to the problem of weak technical assistance. Here assessments of organization performance can yield data to underpin such technical assistance, and

---

[8]*Ibid.*, p. 286.

more broadly to facilitate the larger fixer role. Surely, the agency information strategy needs to be cast in terms of the comparative advantages and limits that derive from these technical and bureau-cratic/political realities.

ACCESS TO INFORMATION

Lots of key actors could use sound, timely organizational and pro-gram information to exert performance pressures. The need is for a freer flow of information, for more access to this general com-modity. Yet information so often becomes a defensive weapon. Governments hide it; the claim is made that there is not time to get it, that those requesting the information really do not need it, or that outsiders will use it improperly because they do not understand it. To be sure, dangers of misuse do exist. But this makes the case for a more intense effort to develop better data, not for suppression. Two instances of the need for more information will be con-sidered—that of field units which administer and operate projects, and that of citizens.

Our field study of CETA and CDBG showed that the agencies often failed to provide useful feedback information from the de-tailed and involved reports they required. The typical case was one where headquarters demanded data without explanation or rationale. Data went up. But apparently in defiance of a basic law of physics, it did not come back down. The implication is that people in the field would not benefit from headquarters's comments on their particular project information or information drawn from other local activities. But if local-level information is not perceived by those above as useful at that level, one must wonder about how it is used at higher levels.

One reasonable deduction is that headquarters lacks a basic understanding of the relationship between information and control. As Anthony and others point out: "The management control pro-cess and the data used in it are intended to influence managers to take actions that will lead to *desired* results."[9] A second explana-

---

[9]Robert N. Anthony, John Dearden, and Richard F. Vancil, *Management Control Systems: Text and Cases* (Homewood, Ill.: Richard D. Irwin, 1972), p. 7, italics in original.

tion is that the headquarters information game is a sham or a "con" to keep external (to the agency) critics, particularly Congress, at bay—a propaganda gambit rather than a means of control, advice, or policy formulation.

Another justification for a freer flow of information is to increase external, marketlike pressures from local citizens who may be voters, parties with a direct stake in a program, or both. Such people bolstered by sound, timely information may be able to exert stronger performance pressures on local governments and operators than the federal government itself. However, providing good information to citizens is even more difficult than providing it within governments.

Historically, federal legislation has been ambivalent about citizen involvement. The New Federalism legislation had the right rhetoric about citizen involvement, yet power was concentrated in local elected officials at the expense of citizen groups while claiming this provided more citizen involvement. Recentralizing power in "city hall" was good, it was argued, because elected officials represented all of the citizens of a geographic area and had to answer to these citizens at election time.

The apparent assumption is that the voting process alone will drive elected officials toward adequate performance. However, the vote alone—as a means of citizen control over social service delivery programs—seems deficient in two ways. First, decisions about social projects that may be critical to citizens may occur any time, but elections come every two or four years. Second, and relatedly, elections are seldom a plebiscite on the efficiency or effectiveness of programs such as CETA and CDBG. Only in rare cases where dishonesty or flagrant mismanagement flare into newsworthy controversy do significant numbers of voters cast their ballots as indicators of concern about particular programs. Basically, this is true of all local programs, especially those funded primarily by federal funds. As such, it is an endemic issue of large-scale democracy when candidates stand for general election.

But how are citizens to participate meaningfully in the decision process for specialized areas such as employment and training or community development? By what means can citizens obtain both sound, relevant, timely information and the technical knowledge to use that information effectively in the local decision process?

Agencies may attempt to aid local citizens gain information about programs *prior* to the making of decisions. Equally important may be technical assistance to help citizens formulate questions about performance and to put pressure on local authorities to come up with answers in understandable language.

The local process is a political one. We should not overvalue information or underestimate the importance of the more pure forms of political power and pressure. Instead, what needs to be recognized is that citizens so often are at a disadvantage in the local decision process. Information resources offer help in this political arena. There can be benefits to the agency in terms of performance pressures through supplying such information and aiding local people in interpreting it or in obtaining information themselves.

FIELD CAPACITY

One of the clearest findings of the CETA and CDBG case studies was the failure of the social agencies to provide useful technical assistance. And these technical assistance weaknesses continue to plague current programs even though *both* the federal and local staffs are well aware of the great need for support services. For example, in the case studies, even the most experienced and competent local staffs, the ones most contemptuous of the support services *actually* received, were quick to point up how much they could use technical assistance on organizational and program problems. The needs of others are even more apparent, as Ginsberg and Solow lament: ". . . the sorry fact is that most state and local governments—with some notable exceptions—are poorly structured and poorly staffed to carry out new and innovative tasks. They have a hard time even meeting their routine commitments."[10]

Reasons for the Technical Assistance Failure

The starting point in considering substantive technical assistance problems is the deficiencies in the underlying knowledge base for

---

[10]Eli Ginsberg and Robert M. Solow, "Some Lessons of the 1960's," *The Public Interest*, no. 34 (Winter 1974), p. 217.

social issues. These deficiencies go far in explaining absolute weaknesses in technical assistance. As has been stressed, nobody knows what to do about a number of problems. But as also emphasized, these difficulties increase the need for federal and local staffs to work together. Information base deficiencies alone do not explain why technical assistance is so poorly delivered.

The primary reason for the relative failure is deficient agency technical assistance strategies. There appears to be an overall imbalance in social agency staff in that insufficient numbers of higher quality people are in the field to deliver substantive technical assistance. The field gets shortchanged on human resources with too few of the available higher level people and/or of the outstanding more junior staff.

The agencies have stretched their technical assistance resources too thin. A good example is the requirement for all local units to participate in regional or area office training sessions even though the better local staffs may have far more capability than the trainers. In light of limited federal field resources and a wide distribution of local government capabilities, the better approach would be to concentrate training efforts by matching resources and needs. The "treat everybody alike" approach produces both resource misallocation and loss of credibility for federal staffs.

The staff imbalance in the field, however, is not purely inadvertent. The field is a dumping ground for unwanted people. As Nathan has observed: ". . . federal officials in the field often tend to be the most rigid and inflexible of program-oriented career officials. Their more creative and innovative colleagues tend to gravitate to Washington; the old liners are the ones typically 'selected-out' for field assignments when changes are sought either within the bureaucracy or from outside."[11]

The Big Shift

The complexity of field problems and the need to work on the spot toward solutions over time point toward a change in the overall personnel distribution that shifts a greater percentage of the more talented and more skilled staff to the field to treat technical assis-

---

[11]Richard P. Nathan, *The Plot That Failed* (New York: John Wiley & Sons, 1975), p. 30.

tance issues. This, by the way, does *not* necessarily mean a greater number of field staff. The concern is with staff quality, not quantity.

The social agency field staff needs better high-level managers, persons with the ability to keep organizations moving toward better performance in the complexity of the field. There also is a real need for more narrow specialists on particular elements of administrative, organizational, and program approaches and procedures. Perhaps those most needed are middle-level staff who can treat broader organizational and programmatic problems. Such people, often labeled generalists, have the ability to synthesize information, to see across projects, to treat an organization as a whole.

In terms of technical assistance, the need is for federal staff who can both aid on specific local management problems and build local managerial capability over time. *The most basic requirement is technical assistance to help local institutions develop the overall managerial capability needed to plan for and cope with future problems.*

A host of organizational issues will be raised if higher quality staff is shifted to the field, particularly with no changes in staff size. Uppermost in the minds of headquarters may be that the reallocation of such staff to the field threatens its capability to handle the "top-level" issues of organizational health, thereby increasing the danger of political explosion.

Even if the initial changes are made, the tendency will be to pull this reallocated staff from substantive technical assistance concerns. The pressures can come from headquarters itself to handle hot issues or from field managers to treat immediate control problems or crises that threaten organizational health. These crises are not going to wither away. So both headquarters and field managers will always be tempted to draw relatively competent staff members into their immediate problems. Over time, the agency well may shift people back to headquarters. The pull will be toward the old quality balance between headquarters and the field. If agency management decides staff should be doing something else, no organizational restructuring will insure a continuing commitment to keep higher quality of staff working primarily or exclusively on substantive technical assistance.

The logistics of better technical assistance is certain to bring organization problems. These organizational issues, however, should not be allowed to obscure the fundamental issue of better technical assistance—the need for greater capability in the field to provide managerial assistance and substantive support services to grantees. Whatever the structural arrangements, and in the whole federal experience almost all organizational structures have been tried, the need to reallocate staff so as to provide greater managerial and staff skill remains. This is the great untried experiment in agency organizational change.

THE LIMITS OF STRUCTURAL REORGANIZATION

In its many bursts of reorganization rhetoric the incoming Carter administration underscored Harold Seidman's claim that "reorganization has become almost a religion in Washington."[12] When there's a big problem, reorganize—shift and consolidate the organizational boxes, move people around, add or subtract functions. Such changes have a tremendous appeal to top management. There has been a continuing belief that we'd get lots more performance out of the available resources, if only the organizational structure made more sense. But how good a means is a structural reorganization—particularly top down changes—in improving an agency's capability to carry out its responsibilities?

The HUD reorganization discussed in Chapter III offers vivid testimony to the difficulties of major reorganizations decreed from the top of the agency. Now let us add more evidence, relying particularly on Donald Warwick's penetrating study of a Department of State reorganization that went wrong. From this experience Warwick has tried to draw some general themes about ways of going about structural reorganization.

Warwick argues that two kinds of organizational change are almost always counterproductive. First are deep staff cuts, which

---

[12]Cited in David S. Brown, " 'Reforming' the Bureaucracy: Some Suggestions for the New President," *Public Administration Review*, no. 2 (March/April 1977), p. 165.

he labeled provocatively as "debureaucratization by decimation,"[13] and observed;

> [Such cuts] will lead to even less risk-taking and to a search for organiza-
> tional defenses against a hostile environment. A reduction in risk-taking
> will mean that more and more decisions are referred to superiors for
> approval, with a consequent strain on their information-handling ability.
> At the same time the battered bureaucrat will seek out other means of
> protecting himself against the threat of dismissal. One might be more
> sharply defined rules about "proper" behavior. Another might be a
> heightened demand for management positions, on the hypothesis that
> managers or administrators are more durable than ordinary bureaucrats.[14]

The most basic strategic error in structural reorganization is the
imposition of the changes from the top. *A reorganization must
make sense both to the agency employees all along the line who
will implement it and to external actors who have a stake in the
outcome.* The latter may include Congress, employee unions,
fund recipients, and anyone else who sees the reorganization as a
threat and has power to do something about it. *But it is the internal
actors who are most critical, and the ones who draw in the external constituents.*

To sell a structural reorganization to the internal constituencies
affected by it requires that the people be brought in early, listened
to about what to do, and finally convinced that the changes are in
their interests. However, significant changes that disrupt people's
lives and lessen status and power simply may not be saleable.
Moreover, early negotiating allows staff to build up defenses or
engage in endless wrangling. Yet, in the long run, it seems better
to abort a structural reorganization than to spring it on the agency
and have it bring endless disruption.

Structural reorganization is a limited tool. It often brings more
harm than good, especially when the change is large and rapid.
The bitter truth is that sound structure alone does not produce
either better management or better staff performance. The "su-

---

[13]Donald P. Warwick, *A Theory of Public Bureaucracy: Politics, Personality
and Organization in the State Department* (Cambridge, Mass.: Harvard University
Press, 1975), p. 206.
        [14]*Ibid.*, p. 208.

perior'' structure on paper may have little or no effect upon a weak management or on an inferior staff that has been moved around but not changed in composition. Indeed, *causality appears to flow from management to structure with poor structure being a symptom of poor or misdirected management rather than the cause of problems.* As Anthony and Dearden observed: ''Good people can overcome the defects in a management control system, but even the best management control system will not lead to satisfactory results without good people to operate it.''[15] Competent managers may be able to effect structural changes over time that both confront basic problems and are not as disruptive as the large, rapid ones.

Warnings about the difficulties of structural reorganization in no way deny that poor organizational structure can inhibit organizational performance. Some situations surely cry our for organizational change. And certainly, organizational changes, justifiable or not, will continue to be made.

I believe that if changes focus less on organizational boxes and more on managerial direction and on functions including the provision of information, there may be some opportunities for gains. This is particularly true in regard to activities in the field. However, we had better be mindful of these reorganization dangers in the upcoming discussion of the agency implementation strategy.

------

[15]Robert N. Anthony and John Dearden, *Management Control Systems: Text and Cases,* 3d ed. (Homewood, Ill.: Richard D. Irwin, 1976), p. 19.

VII
The Agency Implementation Strategy

We now concern ourselves with a social agency strategy of governance that is consonant with the limits of its power (its control and influence) and its organizational resources. The implementation perspective can provide the underpinning for that agency strategy. It can provide the basic directional guide to orient the agency.

The perspective holds that the basic focus of social agency policy should be increasing the commitment to performance goals and the management and delivery capacity of the organizational units actually providing services. This is the central direction for agency policy. Agency organizational actions need to be scrutinized in terms of whether or not they make basic investments in managerial and delivery capacity at the local level more likely.

A clear guiding point that orients agency decisions and action is essential. With so many complex layers of governments and bureaucracy, it is easy to lose the basic sense of direction that should be steering people toward the performance goals of social policy. The most important management guide to those who govern our social service delivery programs is that which turns them away from fundamental misdirections.

Maintaining direction is the basic management responsibility. No organization is going to be able to sustain an implementation effort centering on organizational capability without concerted leadership from the top of the organization. As I have argued elsewhere:

> The attitude of management is the first and by far the most important factor in improving implementation. *Wanting better implementation will go a long way toward achieving it.* But "wanting it" does not mean that top-level management can mouth platitudes about the need for good implementation. Rhetoric is not enough. Management must make the hard choices required to institutionalize implementation as a critical part of programmatic activity.[1]

Here is the point where organizational complexity intrudes. Most of the chapter deals with the difficulties of a social agency in moving beyond the rhetoric of implementation toward organizational efforts that reflect more realistically the field environment in which organizational and program performance will be determined.

THE FIRST BIG STEP

The implementation perspective will force a particular agency to ask hard questions about its *own* underlying commitment and capacity. At basic issue is whether the agency can alter its orientation and style of decision making to develop the resources and the organizational structure needed for *implementing* the implementation perspective.

The immediate need in any particular agency is an extended analysis in terms of commitment, limits, and resources to determine if the implementation strategy makes sense for that organization. *Basic agency decisions should not be made without detailed study and deliberations that include those whose status and jobs will be affected in the organization.*

Lest there be some misunderstanding let me be clear about my argument. On the one hand, I believe strongly that the imple-

---

[1]Walter Williams, "Implementation Problems in Federally Funded Programs," in *Social Program Implementation,* ed. Walter Williams and Richard F. Elmore (New York: Academic Press, 1976), p. 25.

mentation perspective and a viable implementation strategy are needed by *all* social agencies operating in the milieu of shared responsibility. On the other hand, *all* the available evidence indicates both that new orientations toward and styles of decision making are difficult, if not impossible, to impose from above, and that major internal organizational changes cannot be put in place successfully without careful analysis and the involvement of key organizational units in that change process. The only sensible suggestion, then, is for the agency to start the necessary analysis of its commitment and capacity to adopt the implementation perspective and concomitantly an agency implementation strategy.

It would be the gravest error to view the agency analysis as simply a broad attempt to take a philosophical look at changing the agency style. Commitment to be sure does come down ultimately to accepting broad principles and directions. But the agency needs to probe in depth as to what that commitment means. It must ask what kinds of capacity the commitment demands.

THE EXTENDED ANALYSIS

This section will pose the critical issues a social agency should address in an extended analysis of the feasibility of adopting the implementation perspective, and then discuss each issue in some detail. I cannot overemphasize that no effort will be made to try to treat the issues in terms of a specific agency. This analysis, which elsewhere I have called an implementation analysis, is an inside exercise although outside consultants can help.[2] But this is not a task to be contracted out for a glossy report. It must be a serious effort by the agency staff to determine the dimensions of its internal implementation problems. *Indeed, recognizing that*

---

[2]See Walter Williams, "Implementation Analysis and Assessment," in *ibid*, pp. 280–282. Implementation analysis is an effort made *before* the introduction of a new approach or program to determine the feasibility of putting the new activity in place. Implementation assessments are done after an approach or program is launched to see how well implementation has gone.

*adopting the implementation perspective is itself a fundamental
implementation problem is a major step toward reality.*

There are five critical organizational issues to be considered in
analyzing the feasibility of pursuing an implementation strategy.
The agency should investigate in detail through an implementation
analysis the extent to which it can:

1. Make bargaining and fixing the primary guides to agency decisions
and actions in pursuing organizational and program performance objectives;

2. Develop institutional arrangements that reduce the complexity and
confusion in the field experienced by subnational organizations and
increase the credibility of federal field staff to grantees;

3. Raise competence in the field both of federal staff and grantees;

4. Increase marketlike pressure points that guide toward desirable
organizational and program performance;

5. Develop an information process to facilitate the execution of the
agency implementation strategy.[3]

Before looking at these issues, let us consider briefly where a
shift to the implementation perspective would be expected to take
the agency. The final agency goal is heightened program performance. But improved organizational performance is the critical
intermediate step toward improved program performance. The
policy variables the agency has a real chance of manipulating are
mainly organizational ones. Most critical to performance is the
political, organizational, and technical capability of various organizations in the implementation process, particularly the social
service delivery organizations.

The implementation perspective aims at both organizational
commitment and capacity. As to the former, the desire is for
organizational units to seek improvements in their organizational
and program performance as their first objective. A strong commitment to performance is the critical first step, but these organi-

---

[3]The five critical issues and the subsequent discussion of them are drawn from
my forthcoming book *Social Agency Governance*, to be published by Academic
Press. In that book the issues are treated in greater detail than below.

zations also have to be able to do what is needed. Capacity demands institutional investment over time that strengthens organizational responsiveness and technical skills. Organizational health is one important aspect. The need is for a viable institution that can survive in the larger community in which it exists. To forget these political and bureaucratic needs can be fatal, so sound organizational health is a necessary condition for improved service delivery.

Improved organizational performance ultimately demands institutional investment in management and staff to build organizational capacity. What is sought through institutional investment is not the delivery organization's compliance with agency directives, but enhancement of its general commitment and capacity. The goal is sufficient organizational and technical skills of the management and staff of social service delivery organizations in order *both* to exercise reasonable discretion at the point of service delivery and provide the particular services that are required, *and* to respond appropriately to future, yet unspecified implementation demands.

We need to be clear that increasing institutional investment can be both dangerous and frustrating. Much can go wrong. One of the most frustrating paradoxes of building organizational capacity is that the increasing strength of the organization can well lead to bureaucratic rigidity. As organizations grow stronger, their members have more to lose and hence more to protect. On the road to institutional viability, organizational health can replace performance as the organization's main goal. No organizational problem looms larger than that of retaining or renewing responsiveness in organizations as they gain institutional strength.

The implementation perspective has been prescribed as the principal guide to managers. But it must be clear that this guide is not going to tell managers how to treat a particular situation. For example, there will be no specific instructions that indicate what a superintendent should do with school principals or what school principals should do with classroom teachers. Here we have another paradox. On the one hand, it can be said of managerial skills that their main payoff comes at the point where managers make the discretionary judgments that directly affect organizational performance. Managers all along the line must find ways to cope with the specific situations that call forth these discretionary judgments. On the other hand, no notion is more central to the implementation perspective than that precise guidance for treating complex social service delivery problems cannot be delivered in the abstract at a distance removed in time or location from the point of service delivery. It is a fundamental error to press for prepackaged rules in the face of complexity that demands discretionary judgment.

For those who govern social service delivery programs, it must be a sobering thought that they must depend on managers and staff in organizations over which they have no direct control and should not tell these people exactly what to do—that capacity building rather than regulation is the strategy to follow. But this is precisely the direction the implementation perspective takes, and it is a difficult road to be sure. The demand is for new ways of thinking, organizing, and acting by the social agencies if there is to be a viable partnership in the existing milieu of shared governance. We now turn to spelling out the organizational issues the agency must resolve if it is to pursue the tenets of the implementation perspective.

A New Decision-Making and Action Framework

Let us consider generally (again, not in terms of the situation now existing at a particular agency) whether social agencies can change their orientation and style by looking at bargaining and fixing. Bargaining should have much appeal to political executives since the bargaining mode requires many of the skills of the organizational health game. "Implementation games," as Bardach observes, "are political games."[4] In political games action does not depend on command and control or formal planning so much as an

---

[4]Eugene Bardach, *The Implementation Game* (Cambridge, Mass.: The MIT Press, 1977), p. 278.

appreciation of political/bureaucratic reality and commonsense. Agency political executives do not command legislators or White House staff or even middling level members of the Office of Management and Budget. They bargain.

Bargaining skills at headquarters, however, are not enough. Competence in the field is a necessity if the social agency is to be a sound bargainer. Political executives or top-level headquarters staff may be responsible for and actually engage in some direct bargaining. A bargaining package may be hammered out around a table in Washington, or a key headquarters person may head the federal delegation at a local bargaining meeting. Federal field staffs, however, must have a certain level of competence to do needed homework before these bargaining sessions and to engage themselves in the smaller, less formal bargains that will be struck in the field between field staffs and local officials. Without the significant commitment of resources needed to provide technical support in the field for the bargaining game, political executives and field staff simply may not know what to bargain for.

Moreover, bargaining can be a trap if it lures players to emphasize too much the immediate consequences of the deal at the bargaining table. *Good bargaining in the performance game is more than a virtuoso display of political wits in action.* Federal bargaining strategy must not ignore potential field weaknesses. The critical point is that the two bargainers are not like buyers and sellers who go their separate ways after the transaction. Rather, the bargainers are engaged in a continuing relationship where they are also partners, albeit uneasy ones. The bargain is a good one for the federal government if it increases the likelihood that the other partner will move toward better performance. Getting a local organization to overcommit itself in the bargain, even though it fully intends to fulfill that promise, is not a good federal deal.

The federal bargainer must know the playing field including the social agency's own limits, local limits, local needs, and the kinds of resources likely to address those needs. Such knowledge about limits and what resources the locals need is far more important in indicating how the federal government can help in a joint effort than it is in showing what the federal government can wave before the locals as a bargaining chip. The highest level of federal credibility will come when the locals realize that social agency staff is sensitive to this situation of mutual dependency and perceived powerlessness and to its implications in the performance game. This is what can make productive the continuing game with its recurrent bargaining.

Fixing presents even more problems because repairs and adjustments can cut across all domains and range from legislative changes through project repairs. Fixing in broad terms, of course, is being done all the time. What is so problematic is getting a top-level fixer. As mentioned before, Bardach observes of different levels of fixers: ". . . the one that is hardest to come by, is the intervener at the top, the person or persons with powerful political resources."[5]

Asking who at the top is to be responsible for fixing the performance game is very close to the basic question of who is to manage the agency. The latter is a recurrent issue, as Seidman has observed: "[A Secretary's] principal duties involve matters which are unrelated to the internal administration and management of the institution. . . . Minimal time is . . . [available] for managing the department, even if a Secretary is one of the rare political executives with a taste for administration."[6] Seidman, himself going back to a three-decade-old (1948) Bureau of the Budget study pointing out weaknesses at the top of the agency, indicates that since that time there had been a growth in the number of assistant secretaries and an increase in the decision-making machinery, including the Planning-Programming-Budgeting System, but sees no great improvement:

. . . department heads remain the weakest link in the chain of federal Administration. Unless departmental management can be improved, reorganization cannot be counted on to yield more than marginal benefits.

If we are to do something meaningful about the organization and management of the executive branch, we must start first with the department and

---

[5]*Ibid.*, p. 279

[6]Harold Seidman, *Politics, Position, and Power* (New York: Oxford University Press, 1970), p. 134.

agency [bureau] heads. *New approaches are needed—approaches based on what the political executives' functions really are—not on obsolete concepts of what they should be.*[7]

When the same person is expected to handle political issues having implications both up (organizational viability, top-level decisions) and down (organizational and program performance, implementation perspective), the pressures can be overwhelming. There needs to be full recognition by the secretary that his or her duties will not allow fixing. This function has to be "turned loose" by the secretary in the sense of giving it up as a main function, but assigned specifically to a top-level subordinate with explicit recognition of its time demands.

This is the first step toward institutionalizing the fixer role. One fixer, of course, is not enough. Fixers are required at key points in the operating bureau with critical fixing responsibilities in the field. Nor is the assignment of responsibility enough. There remains the commitment of significant amounts of agency resources to support bargaining and fixing in the performance game. But clearly the establishment of the top-level responsibility for bargaining and fixing is the first critical commitment.

Structural Arrangements Supporting Constraint and Credibility

Here we confront again the basic agency power dilemma flowing from the sharing of responsibilities. The social agency must operate with extremely weak controls. There is great difficulty in specifying objectives and standards, and overt sanctions are limited because of political/bureaucratic factors. It is small wonder that top management seems so driven toward tightening up, toward trying to center authority in headquarters, and toward sending out regulation after regulation. At the same time, the field setting is highly unpredictable. Plans and regulations cannot spell out reasonable responses in advance, yet the cost of delay to wait on headquarters will be high. Moreover, proven field tactics are not available. So the basic requirement is for competent people on the spot. They are the ones who can

---

[7]*Ibid.*, p. 135, italics added.

exercise judgment in trying to find successful tactics. They are the ones who can help build local managerial, organizational, and technical capacity over time.

With weak control points and indeterminacy in the field, what headquarters can do to compel, as opposed to influence, behavior is limited. And unfortunately, as we have seen so vividly in the case materials, the power to complicate and to confuse, as well as to harass, is likely to exceed the power to order or to influence.

One source of confusion is that of unclear lines of authority and communication. People in the field need to know who has specific responsibilities. They need to receive clear signals. However, clearer lines of authority and communication are only a small start toward clarity. Other factors are far more important.

A key factor in the field creating complexity and confusion has been a "regulatory" attitude in the social agencies. This regulatory mentality equates control with compliance. And the costs of compliance can be steep. The rules and regulations designed to ensure compliance themselves become a major source of complexity and confusion that require additional directives and more surveillance. The stream of regulations becomes a torrent. Regulation begets regulation—the second one so often needed to correct or refine a first one. Complexity and confusion mount.

The emphasis on compliance can drive out more substantive concerns, leaving the federal staff tending mainly to narrow procedural issues. Moreover, compliance so often brings harassment by the federal staff. The field interaction becomes a game of wits in which the grantee becomes the enemy. It is hardly a partnership seeking delivery capacity. As Elmore has observed:

When it becomes necessary to rely mainly on hierarchical control, regulation, and compliance to get the job done, the game is essentially lost. . . . Regulation increases complexity and invites subversion; it diverts attention from accomplishing the task to understanding and manipulating rules.[8]

---

[8]Richard F. Elmore, *Complexity and Control: What Legislators and Administrators Can Do about Implementation,* Institute of Governmental Research, University of Washington, Public Policy Paper No. 11, April 1979, pp. 27–28, italics in the original.

Another important source of field complexity and confusion is the incongruity between responsibility and authority. Headquarters tends to overcompensate for initial uncertainty of mission by drawing up broad statements of responsibility. The assignment of unrealistic responsibilities is likely to force federal staffs to overact. The flow of rules that elaborate on or counteract existing rules represents a bureaucratic response to responsibility overreach. In this confusion federal staffs lose credibility. Chasing after unrealistic controls, the agency jeopardizes the forming of the belief by local organizations that the agency knows what it is doing and can set reasonable tasks. To avoid confusion and loss of credibility, the agency must keep responsibilities in line with capability.

Now it is true that responsibility in the broadest sense is a political choice. Congress usually sets these responsibilities for the agencies without necessarily giving much thought to whether or not the agency can really do what is specified. But over time the agency can negotiate with the Congress to determine more realistic responsibilities. More importantly, the agency has a great deal of flexibility in defining and refining them. Most of the responsibilities that the agency assumes are not set out explicitly in the legislation or in congressional intent. *Agencies, themselves, appear to be the main culprits in overpromising.*

Telling agency field staff and local organizations that the former are accountable for performing at a higher competence level when they cannot come even close to doing it obviously can be destructive. If the federal field staffs think their superiors take the charge seriously, they may try to operate at a higher—more frenzied—level than is called for under the circumstances. Or, they may try to "close the gap" between responsibility and capability with activities that harass rather than help.

Such organizational behavior poses a severe threat to agency credibility. Local organizations with any understanding of the gap between responsibility and authority will question headquarters's motives or capacity. If the federal field staffs overreact, they also may become suspect. Federal field staffs may work out some kind of accommodation with local organizations which may circumvent federal specifications. But this action itself erodes the local sense of agency believability. The watchword is headquarters constraint.

Constraint can be seen as part of the headquarters search for a credible position in the eyes of federal and local field people. This can necessitate a tactical retreat to stronger ground that reflects the realities of the field game but does not imply an abandonment of legitimate responsibilities in the performance game. The social agency needs to develop greater influence over organizational behavior, not less. What is sought is a strategy of the type Sundquist labeled "deference":

There are many examples, within the federal government, of a policy of deference—but not all are models for emulation. In the case of many programs where funds are distributed among states by formula, deference has meant a virtual abdication of any federal influence at all—a quiet glossing over of inadequate state and local performance. Much is lost, obviously, if the federal government fails to exert leadership. The federal government can assemble expertise that individual communities cannot hope to match. It can collect and evaluate data from many communities. The information and insight of the federal experts must be brought to bear upon the community plans, and the advice growing out of evaluation must be made available. These purposes require an aggressive federal approach but an aggressive attitude is consistent with a policy of deference if the federal influence is achieved primarily through consultative relationships while the plans are being formed, rather than through review and modification or disapproval of the community's proposal afterwards. The one approach is calculated to stimulate local initiative; the other tends to stultify it.[9]

Agency constraint or deference or credibility all suggest a new agency approach. It is one that seeks a viable working relationship between the federal and local partners that emphasizes increasing the commitment and capacity of local organizations. Fundamental to the implementation perspective is the basic agency choice between a stress on compliance and a stress on commitment and

---

[9]James L. Sundquist, *Making Federalism Work* (Washington, D.C.: The Brookings Institution, 1969), pp. 251–252. Similar notions are found in Bernard Frieden and Marshall Kaplan, "Community Development and the Model Cities Legacy," in *Toward New Human Rights,* ed. David C. Warner (Austin: Lyndon B. Johnson School of Public Affairs, University of Texas, 1977) pp. 310–312.

capacity as the central guide to its organizational structure and behavior.

With capacity as the central guide, the search would be for structural arrangements that decrease complexity and confusion in the field, and increase local adaptability and capacity building, agency credibility, and the exercise of reasonable field discretion. The question to be asked of any structural change is whether or not it is likely to bring greater commitment and capacity at the point of service delivery.

Field Competence

No issue looms larger in shifting to the implementation perspective than that of the allocation of staff resources between headquarters and the field. All the evidence indicates the difficulties of exerting *direct* control and influence by having most of the top-level civil servants, the highly trained specialists, and the brighter generalists in Washington. The argument is that on-the-spot staff potentially can make more sensible judgments because of their detailed knowledge of the situation. Being present must be coupled, of course, with competency. The strategy is to deploy better human resources in the field where the action is, and to increase the tools available to support discretionary judgment.

The most obvious approach to improving the staffing situation is to increase the rewards for those in the field. The Coopers & Lybrand report points out: "With only 25% of the total staff, HUD Headquarters has two-thirds of all grades GS-15 and higher, whereas the Field has most of the responsibility for operating the programs."[10] Coopers & Lybrand recommend that more of the high grades be distributed to the field. There needs to be a sufficient upgrading so that top-level field positions are seen as

---

[10]Coopers & Lybrand, *Recommendations for HUD Organizational Structure,* (Washington, D.C.: U.S. Department of Housing and Urban Development, March 1976), p. 10. Federal employees are classified on a scale from GS-1 to GS-18. The grades GS-16 through GS-18 are called super grades and are severely restricted in number by the Congress. Above the GS scale is another classification grouping for the senior political executives up through the secretary (Level I, the highest, through Level V). In a regional office there is likely to be no one at Level V, one or two super grades, and a goodly number of GS-15s heading major activities.

highly desirable career attainments. Also recommended was that a more intensive effort be made to prepare field staff for greater responsibilities through formal training arrangements.

Perhaps even more important are less tangible factors. After all, there are some super grades and a number of GS-15s in the field. But as long as implementation and field administration remain inferior positions in the agency, the better people will be attracted to them at a lesser rate. There must be recognition in terms of status and responsibility as well as money.

Field staff can become the key agency people making important discretionary decisions intended to influence performance. Those in the agency with high career aspirations must see field service both as challenging and as a major route of personal advancement. Only with rewards and status and challenging jobs increasingly in the field can this crucial element be put in place over time. All we know about organizational behavior tells us that better staff must want to be in the field.

There certainly is a need for them. A major Rand study of the implementation of education programs found the lack of local staff capability a crucial barrier to improvement and an excellent place for federal activities. As Berman and McLaughlin observed: "A major opportunity for federal policy to improve the institutional capability of school districts lies in the largely ignored area of local staff development. . . . The success of any practice depends less on the inherent merit of the technology than it does on the *skills and commitment of the user*."[11] One of the major recommendations made by the Rand research group is to establish "a separate categorical effort [that] would provide a clear signal to state and local school personnel about federal priorities; it would imply that the federal government considers local capacity building to be a fundamental need."[12] There must be more field capacity—a better "human resource base" for the positive exercise of discretion. People out there need the knowledge, sensitivity, and confidence to work toward solutions.

---

[11]Paul Berman and Milbrey McLaughlin, *Federal Programs Supporting Educational Change*, vol. *VIII: Implementing and Sustaining Innovations*, Rand Corporation, R-1589/8-HEW (May 1978), p. 42, italics added.

[12]*Ibid.*, p. 43.

Federal Regional Staffs: The Basic Question of Role and
Responsibility

The issues of the agency decision-making framework, complexity and confusion, and lack of sufficient competent staff in the
field, all are crystalized in the problem of the basic relationships
between headquarters and social agency regional staffs. One thing
that is clear from the studies of the CETA and CDBG implementation is that the role and responsibility of regional staffs was
not resolved. Indeed, one of the major sources of confusion in the
field is the ambiguity and volatility of this relationship. Are
regional staffs viewed by headquarters as compliance clerks—
mainly outposts to provide early warnings of threats to organizational health and to check up on the grantees who might not be
following all of headquarters's regulations? Or, are the regional
offices to be an important part of agency management expected to
make significant discretionary judgments in helping local grantees
with specific problems and to provide managerial, organizational,
and technical assistance aimed at helping local organizations
raise their implementation and administrative capacity over time?

The issue of regional office role and responsibility is in part a
question of structure—of organizational boxes and specified
authority and functions. But it goes beyond mere structure to the
central question of the style and orientation of agency governance.
*In the decision about the role and responsibility of regional
offices, the agency political executives are forced to make the
fundamental choice about its management approach.*

The regional offices are the barometer of agency governance.
This is where an implementation assessment would seek desired
changes in organizational behavior. Here it can be seen if the
implementation perspective has been implemented. *Here it can
be determined whether or not headquarters has accepted the
primacy of the field in the performance game by shifting better
qualified staff, by exercising constraint and reducing field confusion, and by stressing advice and capacity over control and
compliance.*

The Search for Marketlike Forces

The overwhelming view of students of government, including the author, is that more marketlike pressure points are needed in social service delivery programs. Whether to shift to vouchers or some other marketlike device that allows social service clients to purchase such services directly from providers of their choice is a basic decision by the Congress and the White House, outside of the range of agency management. At question now is whether the agency itself can find pressure devices to supplement its direct control and influence efforts.

Pressure devices that make technical, bureaucratic and political sense within the existing structure of shared responsibility are difficult to find. As one possible example, providing information to citizens will be considered, a topic already covered earlier in enough detail to keep the present discussion brief.

Outside pressures brought by citizens offer a potential to the agency for indirect influence. Here are people who may be able to leap political barriers insurmountable by the agency. However, if responsible participation is to be built into the local level decision process, there needs to be more useful information available to citizens.

Strong legislative requirements can make information more available. For example, it can be mandated that critical decision-making information available to local officials also be available to citizens *prior* to the time decisions are made. A stronger requirement would be for specific kinds of information, such as performance assessments, to be made available to citizens. As a HEW planning document once observed, first for all revenue-sharing programs and then specifically for educational programs:

This open-records condition forms the basis for enforcement in all SRS [special revenue sharing] packages. Without it, there is little practical distinction between special revenue sharing and general fiscal relief. . . .

All [education] programs will be required to maintain open books of expenses and other information essential to the public evaluation of the program including, where applicable, test scores by school.[13]

The provision of information, however, is not enough. Responsible citizen participation requires substantive knowledge. Technical assistance could be a key factor in increasing capability to use this information.

Consider the issue of outcome evaluations in terms of citizen involvement and technical assistance by asking how citizens might obtain information to help them make more reasoned judgments about program performance in social service delivery programs. Congress can demand that fund recipients support various kinds of evaluations and make that data available. Congress has made such demands upon the social agencies for years, starting in the mid-1960s with the Office of Economic Opportunity, without much real impact. This probably has more to do with congressional will than anything else. There are some strategies that might get us farther than we are now.

One possibility would be to have social agencies execute final outcome evaluations and to make the information available publicly. Here the agencies could occupy a relatively independent status if they themselves are not responsible for final outcomes. It is hard to envision Congress having enough nerve to sanction agency evaluations in support of citizen decision making. Even if it does, local citizens are still going to need technical advice in using the data.

If Congress leaves evaluations to local governments, citizens will need even more technical help in gaining the knowledge needed to prod local governments to do meaningful assessments and to interpret results. The argument becomes even stronger for the provision of technical assistance to raise the capabilities of citizens to make informed substantive comments about social service delivery programs.

---

[13]"Special Issue on the HEW Mega-Proposal," *Policy Analysis,* 1 (Spring 1975), 374, 379.

Information[14]

The implementation perspective dictates a search for different kinds of information to be put to different uses than in the past. For example, bargaining and fixing clearly will establish different data priorities. Repeatedly, it has been indicated that the most pressing needs will be for the softer, richer, process-oriented information to support advice and policy formulation as opposed to control.

Information remains the critical raw material of governance in the agency implementation strategy with even broader uses than presently. It is the most flexible of resources. What the initial analysis must do is cast the information question in terms of the new perspective—seeking comparative advantages that can be found only by looking at technical, organizational, and political limits. An initial analysis will not answer all questions, but my judgment is that we already know a great deal about the limits of information, so that fairly good answers can be determined if the right questions are posed.

A NOTE OF GUARDED OPTIMISM

I have only gone so far as to prescribe that the agencies test the water through an analysis of the feasibility of the agency implementation strategy and to offer a framework for the analyses. Such analyses undoubtedly will show limits and weaknesses but also room for maneuverability. Analysis over time is likely to indicate where organizational change is least threatening and where agency resources have potential for a visible impact. The general expectation is that there are opportunities within the social agencies for getting the agency implementation strategy started and for building an institutional base that will support it. I am guardedly

---

[14]The brevity of this section reflects how extensively the topic has already been discussed, not its relative importance.

optimistic that the social agencies can have success in using their resources to foster a higher commitment in the field to performance objectives and to provide the needed resources to build organizational and technical capacity that will support the exercise of field discretion by those who ultimately determine social policy.

VIII
Summing Up

In this chapter the concept of the implementation perspective will be pursued in two directions. First will be a broad look at the implications for the evolving American federalism. Second will be a brief consideration both of the general relevance of these concepts for all jurisdictions and organizations governing social service delivery programs and of their specific relevance in terms of the current national mood embodied in the balanced budget movement and Proposition 13.

THE EMERGING AMERICAN FEDERALISM

Central to a wider view of American federalism must be a sense of the history of federal grants-in-aid to support social service delivery programs. The Great Society, the New Federalism, the early Carter administration are episodes in the unfolding history of American federalism. It is a period marked by turbulence and change that provides a richness of experience upon which to draw.

However, as we look back on this turbulent and intense activity and its changeability, there is a constant. The nation has made a fundamental choice that the governance of social service delivery programs will be shared. Be the programs funded through categorical or block grants, Congress has continued to dictate the uneasy partnership. Only Congress can dissolve the federal-local partnership, call it bankrupt, and start a new company. And there is absolutely no indication Congress has any such intention.

The argument for developing a strategy that is within the confines of the present approach of shared governance does *not* rest solely on the premise that shared governance is politically immutable. It is far from clear that other approaches hold out more promise than shared governance. That funding arrangement in its complexity reflects the complexity that drives the current system. The legitimate differences between federal and local needs and interests are seldom clear cut and often intertwined, so there is a continuing need to have these interests worked out through the active participation of all the key actors. The federal government needs to have an organization that is in the pivotal spot of linkage between federal and local governments and has the resources required for active involvement in the field to pursue national intent over time.

That role becomes both more crucial and more difficult because congressional intent is usually so unclear and so in need of being developed and negotiated during the process of program activity. As discussed earlier, the Constitution does not require clarity or sharpness or consistency in legislation. Congress can call a spade a number of things. Often this is precisely what it has chosen to do, and what ought to be done. Pressure politics and wisdom seem to combine to render national intent a summation of interests sufficiently broad to allow needed diversity.

Such looseness well may reflect the wisdom of democratic federalism. The checks and balances of our consititutional system produce a rather messy and often conflict-filled setting which offends and befuddles the orderly mind. Yet it may fit the nation's needs better than more rational-appearing solutions.

There are some significant costs, however, that we should be clear about. The looseness that reflects the wisdom of democratic federalism often is bought with the currency of control. Congress can create the *appearance* of tight control (the ''Secretary shall'') while keeping desired looseness. But Congress cannot suspend certain iron laws of control.

Two are critical. The first law is that federal control is at its maximum at the point *prior* to the basic decisions on allocation and distribution. The second is that strict control almost certainly requires both clear boundary or control points and strong sanctions to punish violations. Take an example of the first law. If Congress wants local governments to concentrate on private-sector-oriented training for private sector jobs as opposed to public service jobs in CETA, it needs to restrict local choice by earmarking funds specifically for this purpose. When Congress allocates employment *and* training funds together to local governments and allows them to choose between them, we know pretty well what to expect, since public sector positions are easier to develop and public and nonprofit organizations will cry for such funds.

Congress could take these laws of control more into account in legislation, being both more specific and more willing to enforce sanctions. But generally, and often quite wisely, Congress chooses to ignore these laws. It finds the costs of strict control far too high. However, and I do not believe that this is wise, it approaches the agencies as if the laws of control do not exist, charging them with responsibilities that are not compatible with lack of control. So often Congress violates the basic management principle linking responsibility and authority when it charges the agency beyond what it can do.

It would be nice if Congress would recognize these difficulties. But realistic prescription cannot be based on such an assumption. The agency implementation strategy must be predicated on congressional behavior continuing much as it has in the past. Recommendations must address what the social agency needs to do in this fuzzy, conflicting setting.

Can the agency implementation strategy be pulled off? The call is for both more management capability and major structural changes over time. Not only is the agency asked to exhibit for more subtlety and finesse than in the past in the performance game, but it is also expected to run real risks in the organizational health game because of the shift in resources necessitated by adopting the implementation perspective. The great flaw of the agency implementation strategy may be that too much is demanded of the social agency.

The major organizational changes envisioned in the agency implementation strategy carry the potential for organizational harm, a further weakening of the agency. Nothing guarantees that those at the top of the agency will use reasonable means that both bring those affected by the reorganization into the early discussion and allow sufficient time for working out the new organizational structure. This, as has been pointed out over and over, is not the style of political executives.

The opposite danger is that the agency implementation strategy will make the social agency stronger, and hence more able to interfere in the local process, without increasing its commitment to operate with deference or its recognition of mutual dependency and of the need to aid the local partner in better delivery of social services. The clear and present danger is that increased organizational strength will be employed to seek greater organizational health and security—to force compliance that satisfies bureaucratic power. There is no denying that one outcome of an agency implementation strategy could be greater government intrusion, more agency capacity to pursue compliance over local capacity, rather than a more realistic partnership.

Under the circumstances, it is tempting to call for fundamental changes that take the social agencies out of an active role in social service delivery, reducing them to paymasters. And surely one can find evidence in the last twenty years of experience to support a claim that the uneasy partnership will not be able to cope with the implementation problem in the social service delivery areas. I think it premature, however, to abandon the shared governance arrangement. Matters need to be put into historical perspective. We need to recognize the speed and depth of the changes in American federalism in the last quarter century.

In the case of social service delivery programs, grants-in-aid cover a brief period of less than two decades—a time of national internal turmoil I think unequalled except by the Civil War. The nation has come from ground zero, where either federal and local governments had no program experience in particular areas such as community development or neither had much experience with special programs for the disadvantaged in any of the social service areas. Not only was our knowledge base about these programs small, but even in terms of what we knew, governments at all levels had not made the technical and organizational investments needed to bring capacity up to the current state of the art. Moreover, this working out by inexperienced social agencies and inexperienced subnational governments carried into the murky waters of intergovernmental relations and beyond to basic political issues at the heart of American federalism. It was a new and unknown world of unimagined complexity where reigned mutual dependency and perceived powerlessness—factors so uncommon in the American image. In retrospect it is easy to see how unrealistic were the expectations of rapid innovation and signal improvements in social service delivery programs. Shared governance perturbs too many basic social, political, and organizational forces to expect speedy and orderly institutional adjustment.

I do not claim now that the right adjustments will be made. Nor is it certain that the social agencies can make the needed changes. But I do argue that we have not yet had a fair trial. The nation does not have a firm base of evidence to support a radical shift of direction. Hence, I have called for some tinkering—albeit rather significant tinkering. *The implementation perspective offers the next step in the unfolding saga of the uneasy partnership. It is a step that takes account of the intense history lesson of the past couple of decades establishing a milieu of shared responsibility.*

THE IMPLEMENTATION PERSPECTIVE: A MANAGEMENT GUIDE FOR TODAY

In one sense the claim is quite straightforward that the implementation perspective and the prior discussion above are generally relevant to managing the delivery of social services at all levels of government. We looked at federal grants-in-aid because of both their importance and their institutional complexity that makes for rich illustration, not because of their conceptual differences. Indeed, the fundamental problem of social service delivery programs at all levels of government clearly starts at the bottom end where social service professionals interact with clients or students. Surely, there are few left who think that federal grants to localities with no strings attached or vouchers going directly to individuals for the purchase of services would solve the terribly difficult problems in say the classroom or the job market—that implementation problems in social service delivery organizations would vanish with the removal of the federal hand.

The problems at other levels of government are quite similar to those at the federal level. What was said about overcharging on responsibilities in the last section, for example, applies to most legislatures. At the state level, and sometimes at the local level, shared governance exists with a vengeance. That the state-local partnership is an easier one than the federal-local partnership is far from clear.

Most social service delivery systems are in fact complex, hierarchical organizations with lots of people and bureaucratic layers between the top and the point of service delivery. Not only do the tenets of the implementation perspective apply generally, but I would go further to observe that the discussion of the agency implementation strategy is relevant to most of these large-scale institutions. Here, too, the managers need to adopt the implementation perspective, but not before they have done the hard work of asking the kinds of organization questions spelled out in our discussion of the needed implementation analysis in the last chapter.

Beyond its general appeal the implementation perspective is particularly appropriate in this period of profound disquiet with government. What has been called the "balanced budget movement" in its most general terms seeks to cut back, or at least slow up, government taxes and expenditures.[1] This stress on a balanced budget is a new dimension cutting across the basic federalism issue of the balance of power between federal and subnational governments in the federal grants-in-aid programs. The issue of relative power remains critical, but it may be played out amid dwindling real—and perhaps, even absolute—resources from grants-in-aid. As the Advisory Commission on Intergovernmental Relations has observed after pointing out that grants-in-aid

---

[1]The Spring 1979 issue of *Intergovernmental Perspective*, published by the Advisory Commission on Intergovernmental Relations, entitled "The Balanced Budget Movement: Washington Considers How to Respond," provides a useful summary discussion of the main issues involved in the developing debate over federal budget balancing.

increases averaged $5.9 billion per year for the decade ending in 1978 and $9.4 billion for the final three years of that period:

While the 1979 aid estimate of $82.1 billion indicates a $4.2 billion increase over 1978, it falls far short of such increases in the recent past. Fiscal year 1980 shows a continuing and much sharper slowdown, with federal aid increasing by only $0.8 billion to $82.9 billion. If this estimate holds, fiscal year 1980 will show the slowest rate of growth for federal aid in recent history, with a rate of increase just under one percent. In "real" terms (constant 1972 dollars) this represents an actual decline of $3 billion between 1979 and 1980.[2]

In particular, the social service delivery programs are caught in the budget squeeze. On the one hand, questions concerning America's military capability, its energy crisis, and inflation (with a particular emphasis on health costs) bring new demands on the budget. On the other hand, programs such as Social Security with their legislated entitlements are difficult to cut or even to hold back, in terms of growth. So social services not only have dropped in terms of their saliency in the national debate (and in terms of that debate, well may be a specific target of cuts), but also offer more of an opportunity for cuts than do other programs.

No doubt there is an element of blind budget cutting in the balanced budget movement—a demand for less expenditures without any specification of where the cuts are to come from. But it would be a misreading of current trends in government to see the balanced budget movement as only an exercise in fiscal constraint, to see only a neoconservative call for retreat from government support generally and social commitment specifically. We need to be clear that the call is for a serious debate about the basis of governance itself. And that debate carries to the heart of the management of the vast array of government programs. As David Walker has observed:

These critics of the current federal role in our federal system clearly focus as much on critical managerial, programmatic, structural, political and

---

[2]*Significant Features of Fiscal Federalism: 1978–79 Edition,* (Washington, D.C.: Advisory Commission on Intergovernmental Relations, M-115, May 1979), p. 1.

basic attitudinal concerns as they do on money matters. . . . if the debate triggers a sober sorting out of what managerially, fiscally, and ethically is within the reasonable and realistic reach of the national government, then, in their view, some of the most enervating effects of recent political developments will have been checked.[3]

The implementation perspective—with its central focus on inducing and aiding delivery organizations to make the needed institutional investment to increase capacity—provides that needed managerial direction. It is a most apt guide for governance in this time of budget stringency. A budget cut or slowdown (and often slight absolute dollar increases end up being real reductions in this time of inflation) is itself a particular kind of implementation problem. So often there is organizational shock and a digging in to protect everything then in place. But this need not be the case. It also is a time when adjustments can be made to strengthen basic organizational delivery capability without the pressures of rapid programmatic growth and change. Here is the chance to choose organizational changes—rather than have them thrust upon the organization—with careful attention given to the problems of implementation.

Building greater organizational capability has three potential payoffs. The first, and most obvious, is that the organization will be better able to serve its clients. More efficient and effective service is the only alternative available for increasing actual benefits to participants in the face of declining dollar support.

The second is that better performance could be an important factor in convincing people that social service delivery programs merit additional funds. There is no indication that the United States has decided to turn its back on its social commitments. But the American people do appear to have grown wary of claims of need without some evidence about the capacity to treat those needs.

The third payoff is that improved organizational capacity at the local level will be critical *when* the cycle of spending again turns toward social concerns. Barring catastrophes that drive the nation

---

[3]David B. Walker, "The Balanced Budget Movement: A Political Perspective," *Intergovernmental Perspective,* 5 (Spring 1979), 20.

into distructive war or economic oblivion, the United States will continue to grow. So too will certain of its severe social problems. The pressures for increased spending on social programs will mount even if the needed investment has not been made or organizational and program performance has not improved.

My optimism that social concerns will again emerge as a central policy focus is leavened by my fear that governments will not be building the needed local capability in this time of social retrenchment. A basic message of the implementation perspective is to get on with the slow, hard, unglamorous job of improving the organizational capabilities to provide needed social services. Such a statement in no way denies the hard truth that *nothing* we can do *now* will eliminate implementation difficulties in future social programs. At the same time, nothing can be more clear than that the hard and difficult task of building implementation capacity over time should be done as much as possible before big programmatic increases.

I cannot overemphasize that point. Once the rush of new programs comes, the best that can be done is to worry about immediate implementation problems. Even that is difficult without a solid base of capacity. Now during this period of spending stringency is the time for making the institutional investment in implementation capability—to build the managerial and staff skills needed to respond to the implementation demands made by new, and yet unspecified, directions. If not, the nation again will be unready for rapid expansion of social services. And this time we should be prepared. If we have not learned that lesson, then we have learned little from history of the turbulent period that has just passed.

Appendix
Federal Expenditure Categories

For those not familiar with the federal budget and the classifications of expenditures in it, I have prepared this brief Appendix. To be considered are the budget itself and various ways of classifying expenditures.

The Federal Budget. The federal budget proposed for 1980 exceeds $500 billion. A presentation of that budget runs for hundreds of pages when categories are spelled out in detail. But for our purposes quite a simple classification is adequate. Charles Schultze has divided the budget into these three main categories: payments to individuals, physical investments and subsidies, and social investment and services.[1] Everything else can be classified under a catchall category of "other" where the biggest single item is federal interest payments on the national debt. Payments to individuals (sometimes referred to as transfer payments) are by far the largest category of federal expenditures with social security and public welfare being the most prominent programs. Schultze puts in the physical investment and subsidies category those programs "dealing with the physical or economic environment—agriculture, natural resources, transportation, pollution control, subsidies to business, and science and technology."[2] The final category of social investment and services includes the programs we have been discussing thus far.

---

[1]See Charles L. Schultze, "Federal Spending: Past, Present, and Future," in *Setting National Priorities: The Next Ten Years,* ed. Henry Owen and Charles L. Schultze (Washington, D.C.: The Brookings Institution, 1976), pp. 323–369.
[2]*Ibid.,* p. 335.

Transfer Payments Versus Organizational Service Delivery and Investment.   Transfer payments provide cash or its equivalent to individuals themselves or to a third party usually of the individual's choice (e.g., they pay a medical bill through Medicare or Medicaid). These programs either get resources to individuals to use generally (e.g., social security) or to cover specific broad categories of outlays (e.g., food or medical expenses), but with the specific purchase choice resting with the individual.

Alternatively the federal government may provide funds directly to organizations that serve as intermediaries which deliver services to individuals or make investments. A basic decision is whether or not the federal government should act directly or employ some other organization to engage in these activities. The federal government itself delivers a goodly amount of services from military defense to health care for veterans. In many other cases, and particularly ones we are concerned with, the federal government funds nonfederal organizations in the governmental, nonprofit, and private sectors. The most important category is grants-in-aid to state and local governments. Almost all social service delivery programs are funded through grants-in-aid so that state and local organizations are the primary deliverers of these services that the federal government chooses to support.

Categorical, Revenue Sharing, and Block Grant Programs. Categorical programs specify a particular programmatic approach usually for a defined category of eligibles. Thus, the Job Corps is a residential training program for disadvantaged youth where both the program itself and the eligibility categories are described in detail in the law. In its purest form, revenue sharing simply provides federal dollars to subnational governments with most limited restrictions (sometimes the statement is made that ''no strings are attached'') to support various governmental activities. General revenue sharing provides funds to support general government. What is called special revenue sharing indicates the broad expenditure category such as employment and training or community development in which the funds have to be used. Block grants are intended to be broader than categorical programs in consolidating several categorical grants and so are said to "decategorize" these programs. For example, the Community Development Block Grant program decategorizes seven programs so that grantees receive a *single* grant of funds that can be used at their discretion in the same general program areas. There has been much debate over whether or not there are important distinctions between special revenue sharing and block grants. According to some, a program is special revenue sharing only if it contains almost no restrictions, being like general revenue sharing but with a broad category attached. Block grants are seen as having more restrictions. I will simply refer to all such programs as block grant programs.

A Word of Warning about Classification.   In this paper I point out some of the major changes in the federal budget. If we stick with broad classifications, then we can see important general trends without getting lost in the details of how people such as Schultze decide on specific classifications. Let me give one example to show where confusion may arise. Schultze has chosen to put the public service employment programs, which are a key part of CETA and which I regard as a social service delivery program, under the payments to individuals category rather than social services. This is because he thinks that public service employment programs are nothing more than transfer payments put into salary checks. So his category of social investment and services is both broader than social service delivery and yet excludes some I would put in that category.

I do not want to open the Pandora's box of detailed classification since we do not need to do so for our purposes. The broad trends depicted for social investment and services, social service delivery programs, and grants-in-aid hold whichever of the available classification schemes we might use. That is the important point. We can have a useful general impression of what is happening overall without having to struggle through a detailed analysis of the federal budget.

Index